D1212656

The Conservative Foundations
of the Liberal Order

Defending Democracy against Its Modern

Enemies and Immoderate Friends

Daniel J. Mahoney

Wilmington, Delaware

Library of Congress Cataloging-in-Publication Data

Mahoney, Daniel J., 1960–
    The conservative foundations of the liberal order : defending democracy against its modern enemies and immoderate friends / Daniel J. Mahoney.
    p. cm.
    Includes bibliographical references and index.
    ISBN 978-1-935191-00-1
    1. Conservatism. 2. Democracy. I. Title.

JC573.M35 2010
320.52—dc22   2010020115

Published in the United States by:

ISI Books
Intercollegiate Studies Institute
3901 Centerville Road
Wilmington, Delaware 19807-1938
www.isibooks.org

Manufactured in the United States of America

for my mother

Contents

Preface

I believe that the new self-determination of man can be saved
from destroying itself only by recognizing its own limits in an
authoritative traditional framework which upholds it. Tom
Paine could proclaim the right of each generation to deter-
mine its institutions anew, since the range of his demands
was in fact very modest. He unquestionably accepted the
continuity of culture and of the order of private property
as the framework of self-determination. Today the ideas of
Tom Paine can be saved from self-destruction only by a conscious reaffirmation of traditional continuity. Paine's ideal
of unlimited gradual progress can be saved from destruction
only by the kind of traditionalism taught by Paine's oppo-
nent, Edmund Burke.

—Michael Polanyi, *The Tacit Dimension* (1966)

The Hungarian-British scientist and philosopher Michael
Polanyi wrote the foregoing bracing words on the cusp of
the cultural revolution which did so much to transform the
Western democratic world in the course of the late 1960s and
1970s. The turning point was 1968, a year of immense upheavals in the United States and abroad. Collectively, the events of
that year inaugurated and reinforced a bold cultural and politi-

cal project to sever democracy from the traditional sources of Western civilization. As a result, the noble modern aspiration to uphold the liberty and dignity of all human beings was increasingly disconnected from those goods that gave it substance and moral and spiritual depth.

Henceforth, human relations were understood almost exclusively in terms of contractual relations. Democracy was identified with the single imperative of consent, of choice unbeholden to the inheritance of the past or the goods of our nature. Late-modern democracy has become increasingly estranged from what the French political theorist Philippe Bénéton has called the "common memory, shared references, [and] awareness of a common destiny" that are essential to the vitality and viability of any social and political order, including the liberal one. Such at least was the aspiration of those committed to the comprehensive "deconstruction" of the Western tradition of liberty. This cultural revolution is significantly more advanced in Europe than in the United States, but it has gone a long way toward transforming the American understanding of liberty and democratic self-government. Moreover, as we shall see in the course of our discussion, the doctrine of liberty as liberation, with its project to systematically overcome all external restraints and limitations on the exercise of human autonomy, finds powerful support in some of the core assumptions of modern political philosophy itself.

Twentieth-century totalitarianism represented the most pernicious, willful, and murderous effort to overcome liberal and Christian civilization. The ideological despotisms of the Left and Right left massive physical and moral destruction in their wake and made violence and mendacity their "principle" of existence, to cite Montesquieu's suggestive formulation. In both its Marxist-Leninist and National Socialist forms, totalitarianism entailed a systematic assault on the moral law, the ethical and spiritual traditions derived from biblical religion, and the best heritage of the Enlightenment and modern constitutionalism. Communist totalitarianism revealed to all with eyes to see the folly of human attempts at self-deification. Its record of soul-destroying despotism and systematic lying showed that economic and social "progress" should never be confused with radical emancipation from natural limits and moral restraints and from a transcendent order above the will of men. Communism was opposed by honest conservatives and liberals alike who knew that the West, in both its traditional and modern dispensations, was worthy of allegiance and defense. But, alas, many intellectuals succumbed to the totalitarian temptation—the illusion that Communism represented true human "progress" and the movement of "History"—or gave support to a soft nihilism that contributed to the erosion of the moral foundations of democracy.

Rather than hearkening to Polanyi's call to fortify liberty on the foundations of civilized order, the Western world—and first and foremost its intellectual class—has more and more turned to an idea of "pure democracy" that has little or no place for the crucial historical, political, spiritual, and cultural prerequisites of the liberal order. I call them "the conservative foundations of the liberal order" to highlight that "the conscious reaffirmation of traditional continuity" is the indispensable precondition for sustaining the liberty and dignity of human beings under the conditions of modernity. The reduction of liberty to a vague and empty affirmation of equality and individual and collective autonomy is inevitably destructive of those "contents of life"—religion, patriotism, philosophical reflection, family ties or bonds, prudent statesmanship—that enrich human existence and give meaning and purpose to human freedom.

Consent is a precious principle in the political realm and a necessary protection against arbitrary rule. The "consent of the governed" proclaimed in the Declaration of Independence is a bedrock of democratic liberty. But unencumbered choice can never be the sole criterion for judging the thought and action of human beings. Liberty understood as pure freedom unconnected to larger ends and purposes fatally undermines the dialectics of truth and liberty, and liberty and virtue, that define truly human existence. There can be no liberty without authoritative traditions and institutions, or without openness to the demands that truth makes on thoughtful and morally serious human beings. The "culture of repudiation"—the 1960s-inspired political and cultural project for liberating liberty from the traditions and spiritual presuppositions that have historically supported it— can only culminate in the flattening of souls and the systematic erosion of Western liberty.

In contrast, "liberty under God and the law," to cite Tocqueville's wonderfully suggestive formulation in the final part of *The Old Regime and the Revolution,* stands forthrightly against both the totalitarian negation of man and the "postmodern" identification of liberty with pure freedom or indetermination. It defends what is best in the heritage of Burke—that great scourge of the ideological abstractions of the French Revolution and defender of the continuity of Western civilization—and Paine— the sometimes intemperate defender of "the rights of man"— against those who seem content with humanity sleepwalking into self-destruction through a misplaced emphasis on human self-sovereignty.

This book is an essay in political philosophy and sociocultural criticism. It aims to articulate a thoughtful defense of a conservative-minded liberalism that knows that liberalism has enemies to the left and is not afraid to acknowledge the "conservative foundations of the liberal order." As the political scientist James W. Ceaser argued in his contribution to a December 2009 *National Review* symposium addressing the relationship between conservatism and classical liberalism, conservative liberalism or liberal conservatism (the subtle distinction between the two will become clearer in the course of our presentation) must see beyond liberal theory, whether in its classic Hobbesian/ Lockean or contemporary academic egalitarian forms, since that theory "never developed the tools to sustain itself; it has always required something beyond itself to survive." As the chapters in this book will make clear, that *something* includes openness to "metaphysical" claims about liberty, human nature, and natural justice; a respect for the political framework of democratic self-government, which is the nation-state; and support for "the biblical religions which have been a major source of our ethical system, one of self-restraint and belief in something beyond material existence." A chastened, conservative-minded liberalism also rejects dogmatic egalitarianism and cultivates respect for statesmanship rooted in the best Western and American political traditions. "Greatness of soul" and humility before a natural and divine "order of things" are twin pillars of a humane and civilized order that we ignore or deny at our peril.

This book addresses a wide range of questions related to the theory and practice of liberty. It begins and ends with treatments of exemplary "conservative liberals"—Alexis de Tocqueville (1805–1859) and Raymond Aron (1905–1983). These two great Frenchmen alert us to the nature of the seemingly inexorable "democratic revolution" and the dangers of the totalitarian temptation, respectively. Tocqueville provides the inimitable model of the political thinker and statesman acutely sensitive to the spiritual costs and benefits of the democratic dispensation. He reflected deeply on the political art necessary for sustaining liberty and human dignity in a democratic age where democracy relentlessly democratizes. In his struggle with totalitarianism, Aron concluded that the vigorous defense of Western liberty demanded the renewal of a humane "democratic conservatism" and of those virtues and values—civic courage, prudent judgment, love of truth—that are negated by totalitarianism and soft nihilism alike.

This book also examines statesmanship in a democratic age, the "mutual influence" of religion and democratic liberty, the follies of "pure democracy" and the culture of repudiation, and the reasons for the indulgence of influential modern intellectuals toward various manifestations of totalitarianism and terror. It addresses questions of foreign policy in a manner that seeks to avoid both pusillanimity and doctrinaire support for the spread of democracy abroad.* It attempts to confront the self-destructive tendencies of modernity in a spirit that is conservative rather than progressive or reactionary. The book's dominant tone is analytic and reflective even if it contains a call to thoughtful citizenship and statesmanship. It aims to provide a defense of self-government properly understood against the totalitarian enemies of civilization, both secular and religious, and against democracy's "immoderate friends" (in the words of French political philosopher Pierre Manent), who paradoxically undermine it by promoting its endless self-radicalization. Democracy is

---

* The book only tangentially addresses questions of political economy. An adequate treatment of the subject would demand a different and longer investigation. But suffice it to say that the market economy is not self-sufficient and depends for its successful operation upon virtues—self-reliance, self-restraint, law-abidingness, a sense of fair play—that gain considerable strength from the premodern "moral capital" of Western civilization. Contra certain libertarians and classical liberals, the market economy is not the product of "spontaneous order" alone and is in no way reducible to an amoral "science" that can dispense with human virtue. The writings of Wilhelm Röpke, Bertrand de Jouvenel, and Irving Kristol are particularly helpful for highlighting the moral foundations of the free economy and for exposing the subtle but deep affinities that link individualism in the moral realm and collectivism in the political and economic realms. See my treatment of these questions in chapter 5 ("Economics and the Good Life") of my book *Bertrand de Jouvenel: The Conservative Liberal and the Illusions of Modernity* (Wilmington, DE: ISI Books, 2005).

prone to corruption when its principle—the liberty and equality of human beings—becomes an unreflective dogma eroding the traditions, authoritative institutions, and spiritual presuppositions that allow human beings to live free, civilized, and decent lives.

But there is no reason for despair. As Philippe Bénéton has written, "Modern man is not irrevocably the last man. History is not finished." My book aims to contribute to the revitalization of a tradition of political and spiritual reflection that will allow democratic man to navigate the dangerous waters of postmodern, relativistic democracy. Yet as Ralph Hancock has eloquently suggested, "There is no longer any alternative to exhibiting in broad daylight the hollowness of pure, formal democracy, to plainly stating the dependence of democracy on understandings of human dignity that cannot be extracted from the pure form of democracy."*

---

* Philippe Bénéton, *Equality by Default: An Essay on Modernity as Confinement*, translated with a preface by Ralph C. Hancock (Wilmington, DE: ISI Books, 2004). Because this book aims to be a learned essay that is accessible to citizens as such, I have opted for a minimal note apparatus. But, at the end of the book, you will find "Suggested Readings" for each chapter that reference the principal authors and books under discussion and provide guidance for pursuing its themes at greater length.

Part I

The Art of Loving
Democracy Moderately

1

Tocqueville and the Conservative Foundations of the Liberal Order

This book aims to recover a thoughtful and capacious appreciation of the conservative foundations of the liberal order. Why, then, begin with an examination of the thought of Alexis de Tocqueville? He was after all a nineteenth-century French statesman and political thinker who did not fit within the received political categories of his day, nor ours. He did not share the anti-rational traditionalism of the French and European conservative thinkers of his time, and while he freely called himself a liberal, he hastened to add that it was of a "strange" kind. He is perhaps the most penetrating representative of a French tradition of "sad liberalism." This tradition consisted of chastened liberals who after the French Revolution recognized, however reluctantly, that there was no viable alternative to the new order—modern, democratic, commercial—that was in the process of transforming the Christian European world. They rejected both reactionary nostalgia and revolutionary euphoria, even as they warned against the threats that unbridled democracy posed to the freedom and integrity of human beings.

Among these thinkers, Tocqueville stands out because of his unparalleled insight into what might be lost as well as gained in the transition from the "aristocratic" to the "democratic" dispensations (which he understood as great "orders of humanity" rather than political regimes in the narrow sense of the term). As Pierre Manent has pointed out, Tocqueville's equanimity in addressing the two great "anthropological forms" of political experience—democracy and aristocracy—is rooted in a profound thoughtfulness about human nature and the nature of democracy. Tocqueville acknowledged the justice of democracy and the underlying "similarity" of human beings while never losing sight of the fact that the recognition of the equality of human beings can never substitute for the cultivation of the "grandeur," "independence," and "quality" of the human soul. Joseph Epstein observed in his fine, pithy biographical sketch of Tocqueville that the French aristocrat's endorsement of democracy, while "somehow less than ebullient," nonetheless remained sincere and wise. That sober and qualified appreciation of democracy is an important reason to recommend Tocqueville.

French analysts of the liberal intellectual tradition distinguish between "conservative liberalism" and "liberal conservatism." Conservative liberals have no objection to the fundamental presuppositions of the liberal order (i.e., the rights of man, constitutional liberalism, and the moral and civic equality of human beings) while recognizing the crucial dependence of liberal society upon extraliberal and extrademocratic habits, traditions, virtues, and "inheritances." Liberal conservatives, on the other hand, defend liberty against every form of despotism but are more openly critical of the Enlightenment categories that are used to justify the regime of modern liberty. They more forthrightly reject the illusions of modernity—including the affirmation of the individual and collective "autonomy" or "sovereignty" of human beings, the drift toward indiscriminate relativism, and the "blind worship of progress that destabilizes society, undermines virtue, and tempts modern man with utopian ideologies that lead to totalitarian systems of government," to quote the political theorist Robert Kraynak. There is, of course, no absolute line that separates "liberal conservatism" from "conservative liberalism." Most conservative-minded liberals also criticize the contemporary confusion of liberty with moral relativism and point out the laxity of the progressive-minded before the totalitarian temptation. In the context of his time, Tocqueville may not have called himself a conservative. But in decisive respects he matches the description of both a "conservative liberal" and a "liberal conservative." He was a perspicacious critic of radical modernity *avant la lettre* and the most insightful analyst and judicious critic of the "democratic dogma" (Tocqueville's phrase) that continues to erode the moral foundations of democracy.

Tocqueville had an almost prophetic foreboding that the traditional moral and cultural underpinnings of the free society, the fundaments of civilized order (or the "laws of moral analogy" as he called them in the "Introduction" to volume 1 of *Democracy in America*), would continue to erode under our feet. It would be difficult to gainsay his insight. The "acids of modernity," as Walter Lippmann called them in 1929, continue to do their work. There is seemingly no end in sight to the self-radicalizing propensities of modernity, including modern democracy. In Harvey Mansfield's laconic formulation, "democracy democratizes."

Tocqueville's understanding of the "democratic revolution"— "providential," to be sure, but also relentless and self-radicalizing—provides the larger framework in which the contingencies of our political and intellectual lives unfold. In addition, his writings provide important guidance for preserving the "moral contents of life" amidst the unending democratic storm. In analyzing democracy, Tocqueville wishes to convey to his readers (in his own inimitable words) "the salutary fear of the future that makes one watchful and combative, and not that sort of soft and idle terror that wears hearts down and enervates them." At the conclusion of his penetrating 1982 book *Tocqueville and the Nature of Democracy*, Pierre Manent writes that the lesson to be drawn from Tocqueville is that "to love democracy well, it is necessary to love it moderately." That, I would like to suggest, is the heart and soul of a distinctively conservative, as opposed to reactionary or progressive response, to the challenge of democratic modernity.

AMERICAN THEORY AND PRACTICE

To be sure, Tocqueville is not the only estimable resource for the "politics of prudence" within modern democratic societies. Far from it. The American tradition of statecraft and political thought is rich in theoretical and practical wisdom, especially regarding the art of self-government and the nature of legitimate governmental authority within a federal republic. The American constitutional order's ingenious melding of republican self-government and liberal constitutionalism is one of the most impressive political achievements of the modern world. The American founders admirably affirmed the fundamental equality of all human beings, an affirmation that was honored in the breach but that gave powerful support to the struggle against slavery, the great stain on America's national honor. At the same time, they were wary about dogmatic egalitarianism and utopian projects of any stripe. Conservatives, like other Americans, honor the founders' achievement and are more likely to show deference to constitutional forms. They are rightly suspicious of nebulous appeals to a "living constitution." Fidelity to the founders' constitution remains an integral part of any authentically American conservatism.

But there are important limits to any unqualified "return" to the founding, since the architects of the American experiment in self-government arguably built better than they knew. In Walker Percy's words, they presupposed a "hodge-podge anthropology" that drew unevenly upon classical and Christian wisdom, on the one hand, and Enlightenment presuppositions, on the other. In many ways this was a fruitful tension. But it was also an unstable mixture that was likely to decay as time went on.

Once again this fact was manifest to alert foreign visitors and observers. The French Dominican Raymond-Léopold Bruckberger argued in his eloquent and discerning 1959 book *Images of America* that the genius of America was to recognize the difference between self-government "under God and the law," as Tocqueville put it, and the monstrous illusion that human beings have the "right to deify and worship themselves." At the heart of the "political theology" of America as embodied in the Declaration of Independence (a document that was itself a compromise between Jefferson's rather doctrinaire deism and the more theistic convictions of the members of the Continental Congress) Father Bruckberger saw a wisdom that avoided the twin extremes of theocracy and religious fanaticism at one pole and atheistic fanaticism at the other. For Americans, "the people are always subject and at the same time free and sovereign. They are subject to their own law and God's justice. They are free because they obey their own laws. They are sovereign because their sovereignty is part of the sovereignty of God." To the extent that Americans—and in particular American intellectuals—have redefined their liberty as human self-sovereignty, as pure liberty unbeholden to ends or purposes outside the human will itself, they repudiate their own genius and unknowingly endorse a principle at the heart of twentieth-century totalitarianism.

In confronting willful claims on behalf of human autonomy, it is necessary to remain faithful to the "genius" of the founding while moving beyond the founders' somewhat constricted theoretical horizon. As Orestes Brownson suggested long ago in *The American Republic* (1865), the founders' practical achievement was in decisive respects better than their theory. On the theoretical plane, they endorsed social-contract theory, the conceit that the political community is an artificial construct of free and equal individuals who voluntarily depart what Locke called the "inconveniences" of the "state of nature." However, they were not fully aware of all the metapolitical implications of this doctrine. As Tocqueville appreciated, it could be applied to every aspect of human life and even to the governance of the cosmos itself. But as wise and prudent statesmen the founders respected America's unwritten or "providential" constitution, the habits and mores of the American people so eloquently described by John Jay in *Federalist* 2, as well as the "territorial" character of American democracy. As Roger Scruton argued in *The West and the Rest*, they appreciated that there was a preexisting "We"—a people with certain habits and traditions—that was the crucial precondition for forming a "more perfect union" at the time of America's constitutional founding. They also drew upon the common law and the larger moral inheritance of Western civilization. Unlike the French revolutionaries, they did not and would not start from scratch.

It is up to us today to theorize their practical wisdom and thus transcend the limits of some of their theoretical assumptions and presuppositions. In a particularly illuminating discussion in their introduction to their translation of *Democracy in America*, Harvey C. Mansfield and Delba Winthrop argue that one of Tocqueville's most penetrating insights was that American practice, which includes its prodigious associational life, its rich traditions of local self-government, and its unforced efforts to combine "the spirit of liberty" and "the spirit of religion," was superior to democratic theory. This was "partly because some aspects of American practice had not yet been been transformed by democratic theory, partly because practice tends to correct theory." The American founding is not reducible to modern "theory." But nor is it exempt from some of theoretical modernity's more problematic claims and assumptions.

6

BURKE AND OUR PRESENT DISCONTENTS

As I have suggested, Tocqueville is indispensable for this dialectical rethinking of the theory and practice of modern democracy, for a renewed appreciation of the conservative foundations of the liberal order. What, then, of Edmund Burke? The great Anglo-Irish statesman and political philosopher had a legitimate pride of place in post-1945 conservative reflection on the "politics of prudence" appropriate to modern circumstances. Not only was Burke the inspiration for the "new conservatism" of the 1950s—the conservatism of Russell Kirk, Peter Viereck, Ross J. S. Hoffman, and Robert Nisbet—but he was also recognized as the paradigm of statesmanlike prudence by no less a figure than Leo Strauss. In his remarkable essay "Consistency in Politics" from his 1932 collection *Thoughts and Adventures*, Winston Churchill (a Burkean conservative in his own right) paid eloquent tribute to the "Burke of authority" and the "Burke of liberty," the friend of American liberties and the scourge of French revolutionary fanaticism. Burke's seemingly contradictory public faces were, Churchill argued, two perfectly complementary manifestations of the same animating purpose: the defense of civilization and ordered liberty. "No one can read the Burke of Liberty and the Burke of Authority without feeling that here was the same man pursuing the same ends, seeking the same ideals of society and Government, and defending them from assaults, now from one extreme, now from the other." Burke was the very model of the prudent and "consistent" statesman. No conservatism worth its salt can ignore Burke's incisive defense of tradition and practical reason and his salutary efforts to root modern liberty in the larger inheritance of Western civilization.

In addition, Burke remains a most penetrating critic of the revolutionary or ideological abstractions that risk subverting the

7

achievements of modern civilization. His critique of the pro-totototalitarianism that he saw at work in revolutionary France foreshadowed the more radical and consistent nihilism repre-sented by the Communist revolution in the twentieth century. He opposed the Jacobin revolution with the same courage and singleness of purpose that Solzhenitsyn opposed Communist totalitarianism in our time. Who can forget Burke's profound evocation in his valedictory *Letter to a Noble Lord* (1796) of a new kind of revolution, "a complete revolution . . . extended even to the constitution of the mind of man"?

This "Old Whig" remains a teacher and inspiration even if he belonged in decisive respects to a transitional world between the remnants of the European old regime and a fully modern dem-ocratic order. Burke could not imagine a "perfect democracy" that was not a disguised tyranny. But we live in such a demo-cratic world, one where prescription and established hierarchy have no place in our official political or moral self-understand-ing. We live in a world dominated by the "democratic dogma," which asserts the natural equality and independence of all. To be sure, Tocqueville's thought owed much to Burke: his critique of revolutionary fanaticism, his attack on the irresponsible "literary politics" of French intellectuals, his insistence on the importance of "aristocratic inheritances" such as family, religion, and local self-government to the health and well-being of modern democ-racy are deeply indebted to his great predecessor. Yet the French political thinker praised the practical wisdom of Burke while crit-icizing him for being blind to the full import of the "democratic revolution" unfolding before his eyes. As Tocqueville put it with a certain severity in *The Old Regime and the Revolution*, Burke thought the French revolutionaries had torn apart a living body, when in fact they had assaulted a corpse.

Unfortunately, Burke has lost much of his appeal, even for conservatives. His style is excessively ornate for democratic tastes and his grandiloquent defense of the "gentleman" seems arcane in an egalitarian age. As a result, his books don't sell the way they used to and appear to have little appeal outside the small quarter of traditionalist conservatives. Some so-called conservative intellectuals rather perversely cite the authority of Burke to justify a slow-motion accommodation to the progressivism of the age.[1] Since abortion on demand, the transformation of marriage to include all "consensual" relationships, and various forms of expressive individualism undoubtedly have deep roots in contemporary culture and society, conservatives are called upon to abandon all resistance to the cultural revolution that is in the process of radically transforming the Western world. Conservatism is defined as prudent accommodation to the inevitable. And what is "inevitable" is best discerned by those committed to ever more radically consistent applications of equality and autonomy. But when Burke reminded his contemporaries that "prudence is the god of this world below" he surely did not mean that the "moral constitution" of the universe was subject to fundamental revision. Burke remains our contemporary, but his wisdom needs to be supplemented by sober awareness that the goods he defended need a different articulation in the context of a world where democracy relentlessly democratizes.

At the end of his remarkable if little-known 1957 essay "Concerning the Right: Conservatism in Industrial Societies," the distinguished French political thinker Raymond Aron spoke suggestively of the two ways in which Burke's polemics against the French Revolution can be read today. "They can be read as definitive condemnations of political rationalism—or of ideological fanaticism. As a defense and illustration of the hierarchy of the Old Regime in its particularity or as a demonstration that all society implies a hierarchy and only prospers in the reciprocal respect of rights and duties. Burke has either pleaded against democratic ideas, or for prudence." In my judgment, the second reading of Burke suggested by Aron points in the direction of Tocqueville's conservative-minded liberalism. It thus brings to light the deeper complementarity of Burkean and Tocquevillian wisdom despite Tocqueville's failure to fully acknowledge his debt to his predecessor.

BEYOND THE SELF-SUFFICIENT INDIVIDUAL

Tocqueville's liberalism has little in common with the natural-rights liberalism of Thomas Hobbes and John Locke, who see in liberty above all an *instrument* for the preservation of the lives and property of individuals who are in no essential sense "political animals." Of course, Tocqueville never questioned the desirability of democratic liberties or rights themselves. He was a principled and proud defender of political liberty. But he made clear that the effort to sustain a society based upon the "dogma" of the self-sufficient *individual* is bound to fail because it does not do justice to the nature of man or the requirements of genuine social life. In the words of the Hungarian-born moral and political philosopher Aurel Kolnai, Tocqueville appreciated that the well-being of the liberal democratic order is dependent upon "pre-liberal traditions" that are "ideally negated and condemned by the very conception of man's unlimited self-sovereignty." Tocqueville expressed concerns about the maintenance of these pre- or extraliberal traditions and habits precisely because the democratic notion of popular sovereignty or consent does not limit itself to the political realm. As Tocqueville states in volume 1 of *Democracy in America*, the dogma of popular sovereignty "regulates the greater part of human actions" and thus transforms family life, religion, and other inherited institutions in ever more "democratic" or individualistic directions. Tocqueville was certainly no speculative philosopher but he had

10

already observed what Kolnai states in more explicitly philo-sophical language in his 1949 essay "Privilege and Liberty":

> The liberal-democratic social order reposes on axioms, con-ventions, traditions and habits (whether they be expressly held or tacitly respected) which transcend the liberal-democratic framework itself and impose certain "material" or "objective" limits on both individual and popular sover-eignty, thus helping to maintain a kind of accord among the multiple individual "wills"; between the free citizenship of the individual on the one hand, and the "General Will," as monistically embodied in state-power, on the other.

Tocqueville was completely devoid of progressivist illusions. He did not believe that the "providential" or "fated" character of the great "democratic revolution" unfolding before his eyes in any way *guaranteed* that the new dispensation would preserve the liberty and greatness of human beings. That depended on the prudence of men, on the "art of liberty," whose task was to preserve the conditions that made possible serious thought and noble and generous action. Tocqueville was a critic of the demo-cratic dogma insofar as it was linked to the unreflective *passion* for equality. But he was a friend of the Christian and democratic affirmation of the dignity inherent in the human soul as such. In this regard, it is worth returning to his dialogue with Arthur de Gobineau, the French diplomat and theorist of scientific racism with whom Tocqueville carried on a remarkable correspondence between 1843 and Tocqueville's death in 1859.

Gobineau and the Limits of Fatalism

Gobineau, eleven years younger than the author of *Democracy in America*, was in many respects Tocqueville's protégé. Tocqueville was impressed by Gobineau's intelligence and erudition and in 1842 commissioned him to assist him on a (never completed) project to uncover the roots of modern morality and a distinctively modern moral sensibility. When Tocqueville became foreign minister of France in 1849, Gobineau served as his assistant and shortly thereafter attained a position in the permanent diplomatic corps. Tocqueville had genuine affection for Gobineau and did everything he could to promote him professionally, but he detested the scientism and racism that informed every page of the latter's multivolume *Essay on the Inequality of the Races*. In a letter to Gobineau (November 17, 1853) written shortly after the publication of the *Essay*, Tocqueville denounced the "monstrous fatalism" that informs all modern racial theories. Gobineau denied the moral (and "physical") unity of the human race and wrote off whole peoples as "degenerate," incapable of moral improvement or participation in the benefits of civilization. Tocqueville saw in Gobineau's theories a secular materialist form of "predestination," one that led to a "vast limitation, if not a complete abolition, of human liberty."

Tocqueville judged moral and political doctrines not only by whether they were theoretically plausible but also by their likely effects on the self-understanding and souls of men. In the same letter Tocqueville wrote that while he was convinced that Gobineau's doctrines were almost certainly false, he was certain that they were pernicious. Such "probabilistic" judgments are, with rare exceptions, the only ones available in political life, according to Tocqueville. At a time when Tocqueville was studying German in order to aid his archival research for *The*

Old Regime and the Revolution, he wryly noted that he had "not yet become enough of a German to be captivated so much by the novelty or by the philosophical merits of an idea as to overlook its moral or political effects." He predicted that of all European peoples the Germans alone would provide Gobineau with a favorable audience. More than one commentator has noted the tragically prophetic character of this observation.

Tocqueville despised Gobineau's racialist fatalism because it denied human beings the liberty that enables them "to better themselves, to change their habits, [and] to ameliorate their status." He believed that Gobineau's racialism-scientism reinforced "all the evils produced by permanent inequality: pride, violence, the scorn of one's fellow men, tyranny and abjection in every one of their forms." These words are worthy of much reflection. They capture Tocqueville's deep awareness of the limits of aristocracy if it is shorn of Christian deference to the moral law and a humanizing recognition of the dignity of every human soul. Tocqueville and Gobineau continued their dialogue on these themes for several more years with Gobineau trying without success to convince Tocqueville both of the merits of his thesis and its compatibility with traditional Christian doctrine.

THE REFUSAL TO DESPAIR

At a certain point, Tocqueville (who never lost his affection for the *person* of Gobineau) had had enough. In a beautiful letter dated January 24, 1857, one of the most memorable in the entire Tocquevillian corpus, Tocqueville declared Gobineau's position anathema, incompatible with the "letter and spirit" of Christianity, which clearly affirms "the unity of mankind," and with decency and good sense. In the second part of the letter, Tocqueville asked for permission to no longer discuss Gobineau's political theories. He accompanied this request with a systematic indictment of Gobineau's thought. He argued that a profound contempt for his fellow men informed Gobineau's reflection on modern society. The "very constitution" of man, bereft of freedom of will and all prospects for moral self-improvement, condemns him to servitude, in Gobineau's view. In stark contrast, Tocqueville announces his refusal to despair of his fellow men. If Gobineau affirmed the inevitable "degeneration" of European peoples (who had fatally intermixed with allegedly "inferior" races), Tocqueville insisted that "human societies like individuals become something only through the practice of liberty." In this context, he reiterates his long-held concerns about the difficulties of establishing and maintaining liberty in democratic societies. But he adds that he would never be so presumptuous to think such a task impossible. In the penultimate paragraph of the letter, Tocqueville reaffirms his Christian and liberal convictions against the cruelty espoused or encouraged by what might be called "the atheism of the Right." It would not be anachronistic to see in this splendid affirmation of human liberty and the goodness and justice of God a critique of Nietzsche's position *avant la lettre*. Tocqueville's beautiful *cri de coeur* is worthy of extended citation:

> No, I will not believe that this human species, which is at the head of visible creation, should become the debased flock that you tell us it is and that there is nothing more to do than to deliver it without future and without recourse to a small number of shepherds who, after all, are not better animals than we are and are often worse. You will permit me to have less confidence in you than in the bounty and justice of God.

In the same letter Tocqueville told Gobineau that he took a "profound and noble pleasure in following" his "principles," the principles at the foundation of his refusal to despair of the human capacity for liberty under God and the law. Earlier, in an important letter to his friend Louis Kergolay dated December 15, 1850 (the letter in which he first outlined the great literary project which became *The Old Regime and the Revolution*, his unusually eloquent exploration of the continuities and discontinuities between the old French monarchy and the revolutionary order that swept it away), Tocqueville stated the nature of those principles. They transcend the great historical divide between the "aristocratic" and "democratic" dispensations. Tocqueville told Kergolay that the "forms" that are called "constitutions, laws, dynasties, classes" have "no existence in my eyes, independently of the effects they produce. I have no traditions, I have no party, I have no *cause*, if not that of liberty and human dignity." Tocqueville's fidelity to human liberty was more fundamental than his attachment to a democratic or aristocratic social state, not to mention monarchical or republican political forms.

The Intrinsic Benefits of Liberty

Many scholarly books and articles, some of the highest quality, have been written to elucidate Tocqueville's noble if enigmatic conception of liberty and human dignity. We have already seen that it has next to nothing in common with—in fact it contains a radical critique of—the contractualist liberalism of Hobbes or Locke with their speculative positing of the original freedom and equality of human beings in a prepolitical "state of nature." Human beings escape the "inconveniences" of the state of nature (threats to life, limb, and the prospects for "commodious living" that result from the absence of an overarching political authority) for the sake of security and what the political philosopher Leo Strauss has called "comfortable self-preservation." Tocqueville belongs to an altogether different moral and political universe. In a celebrated passage in the third chapter of the third book of *The Old Regime and the Revolution* ("How the French Wanted Reforms before They Wanted Freedoms"), Tocqueville warns that "whoever seeks for anything from freedom but itself is made for slavery." Tocqueville elsewhere recognized that the doctrine of "self-interest well understood" is a useful instrument (or conceit) for taking democratic men outside of themselves, for reminding them that they live in society and have obligations to other human beings. But it is far from ennobling, and risks turning freedom into a mere instrument, as if it is only useful for the material goods it tends to produce in the long run. Tocqueville defends and might even be said to have personally embodied a view of liberty that emphasizes its intrinsic attractions "independent of its benefits."

In the same chapter, Tocqueville speaks of "the pleasure of being able to speak, act, and breathe without constraint, under the government of God and the laws alone." We need to take seriously every part of this phrase including the invocation of government under "God and the laws." Tocqueville's conservative liberalism unites pride in the human capacity for self-government and the rejection of every form of servility and dependence with a humanizing recognition of limits and the need for self-restraint. The rejection of divine and natural limits leads only to the abyss and in no way allows man to transcend himself. Tocqueville's well-known "aristocratic" defense of human greatness is inseparable from a Christian recognition of common humanity and the recognition of the fact that liberty is always "under God." On the other hand, this "pure love of liberty" eloquently invoked in *The Old Regime and the Revolution* cannot be universalized: it is a "taste" of rare souls who have had it instilled into their "great hearts" by God himself. This admirable quality of soul is not reducible to either aristocratic privilege or democratic equality. It transcends both while being necessary to sustain the love of freedom—and the full range of human possibilities—in any lawful or self-governing human community.

The "Probabilistic" Defense of Human Freedom

Tocqueville decried philosophical systems, like those of the "pantheists" and "democratic historians" he took to task in volume 2 of *Democracy in America*, that had no place for the human element, for the role of human choice and action in helping to shape the course of history. He was firmly convinced that men were beings with souls and in no way reducible to "matter in motion." In his view, their souls were degraded by "false and cowardly" doctrines that made them playthings of either the historical process or of subpolitical determinants such as "race, soil, and climate." He would be deeply suspicious of contemporary efforts to root conservatism in a Darwinian social ethic that reduced human beings to natural impulses shared with other primates and hardwired into us by the evolutionary process. Such "Darwinian conservatism" undercuts human pride, understates the human capacity for independent moral agency, and recovers natural limits at the cost of the human soul itself.

Tocqueville's efforts to avoid the twin extremes of an exaggerated rationalist or utopian confidence in mankind's efforts to transform the world, on the one hand, and of pessimistic or fatalistic denials of human freedom, on the other, can provide guidance for our own efforts to conjugate the relative place of freedom and limits within both the "order of things" and what Tocqueville himself called the "fatal circle" of modernity. In thinking about these matters, we can take inspiration from Tocqueville's "probabilistic" approach. It is superior to every form of scientism and radical skepticism as well as to misplaced efforts to find metaphysical certitudes where there can only be more or less *reasonable* judgments and affirmations. For Tocqueville, one could not so much disprove various forms of historical and racial determinism as show their implausibility as well as their deeply pernicious effects on liberty and the human soul.

SOFT DESPOTISM

Tocqueville's broadly Christian democratic approach informs even his famous opposition to "tutelary despotism." The penultimate chapter of *Democracy in America* ("What Kind of Despotism Democratic Nations Have to Fear") is often misread as entailing an endorsement of libertarian assumptions and opposition to any form of the welfare state. These readings are incorrect. In truth, Tocqueville traces the origins of modern collectivism to a radical individualism that dissolves human connections and makes men dependent on an impersonal "schoolmaster" state. He fears that such dependence will enervate the human soul and destroy the capacity for individual initiative and moral and civic judgment. Carried to its logical conclusion, a tutelary state would deprive democratic man of his very humanity, sparing him "the trouble of thinking and the pain of living." This is Tocqueville's famous nightmare, one *possible* outcome of the democratic adventure.

Writing in the mid-1960s, Raymond Aron, who played a major role in the French rediscovery of Tocqueville after World War II, argued that Tocqueville's portrait of a "democratic despotism" where enervated human beings are subjected to a power that is "absolute, detailed, regular, far-seeing and mild" was "a combination of prophetic insights, excessive fears, and obvious errors." For Aron, the "despotic" aspects of contemporary democratic life were "sufficiently incomplete" for Tocqueville's portrait to be anything other than a salutary warning against certain *tenden-*

cies, never perfectly realized, within democratic societies. In later writings, Aron drew upon Tocqueville's analysis to warn against the erosion of the political instinct in Western Europe, the loss of the spirit of manly independence and civic and martial *virtù* that are necessary even for a regime of liberty. Nonetheless, Aron did not believe that Tocqueville's famous warning would ever provide an exact description of the European present or the American future as long as the Western democracies remained societies capable of self-criticism and independent initiative and open to the "art of liberty" in however diminished a form. Today, this is true even of that excessively administered state and society that is democratic France.

DEMOCRACY VERSUS SOCIALISM

Tocqueville feared not only "tutelary despotism" but also more radical forms of socialism where the state became the proprietor of men and things. In his little-known "Speech on the Right to Work" of September 12, 1848, in which he opposed a constitutional measure to make the government the obligatory employer of last resort, Tocqueville attacked socialism for making of man "an agent, an instrument, a number." He denounced it for its "energetic appeal to man's material passions," its "unending and continuous" assault on the "principles of individual property," and for its confiscation of human freedom. In words that became the inspiration for the title of Friedrich Hayek's famous book, Tocqueville wrote that "if . . . I had to look for a definitive general conception to express what socialism as a whole appears to me to be, I would say that it is a new form of servitude." Using language that is familiar to readers of *Democracy in America*, Tocqueville identified democracy with "equality in liberty" and socialism with "equality in penury and servitude." He wished for his native

France to extend the sphere of citizenship and individual independence as widely as possible, and not to "constrict" it in the
manner that was common to both the partisans of socialism and
the paternalistic "old regime."

In the same speech, Tocqueville insisted that it is necessary to
"introduce charity into politics," to "develop a higher, broader,
more general idea than that previously held of the State's obligations to the poor, toward the suffering." To be sure, in texts like
"The Speech on the Right to Work" and the "Memoir on Pauperism" (1835), Tocqueville worried about the dangers of dependence that flowed from public assistance and recommended doing
everything when designing such programs to preserve individual responsibility and initiative. But he endorsed public charity,
"Christianity applied to politics," as he called it, and firmly dif-
ferentiated such an approach from socialist efforts to make men
mere wards of the state. He announced to his contemporaries that
the French revolution of 1848 "must be Christian and democratic;
but it must not be socialist." Far from being a libertarian doctrinaire, Tocqueville in his writings and example provided a moral
inspiration for an intelligent conservatism that never confuses
public charity or social obligation with socialism or collectivism.
On these issues, too, he remains our contemporary.

CONCLUSION

Let me end more or less where I began. *Democracy continues to
democratize.* Today, in the name of fidelity to democratic principles, in the name of maximizing human rights, democratic activists and theorists alike tell us that we must redefine the nature
of marriage, weaken national sovereignties, defer to judge-made
law at home and abroad, and look with suspicion on all traditional and authoritative institutions. Questions that ought to be

subject to vigorous public debate and discussion are swept aside by intellectual elites in the name of an ill-defined but purportedly all-powerful "democratic" imperative. Nothing should be allowed to get in the way of the "idea" of democracy, the maximization of equality and individual autonomy.

But we immediately confront a paradox: in the name of this abstract "idea of democracy" we are encouraged to abandon self-government to what Pierre Manent calls a vision of a "kratos" without a "people." In the form of the European Union, such a vision of democracy weakens national sovereignty and the concrete expressions of self-government within the territorial nation-state. In the United States, the rule of the abstract idea of democracy takes the form of the judicial transformation of law and politics as well as certain kinds of bureaucratic heavy-handedness. The pressure builds to defer to elite opinion, to the requirements of humanitarianism and egalitarianism, to the moral authority of international law.

In contrast to the tyranny of such an abstract democratic "idea," Tocqueville teaches us to practice the *art* of liberty within democracy and to defend the broader inheritance of Western civilization. The democratic order is not self-sufficient and depends upon a precious civilizational inheritance that it has trouble renewing and that it sometimes actively undermines. With no hope of simply resolving the "problem" of democracy, we must draw upon its *practice* to correct its *theory.* But we must do so in the awareness that there is a tension in the very idea of "popular sovereignty" between the abstract idea, always tending toward more radical interpretations and applications, and the concrete exercise of democratic self-government. Instructed by Tocqueville, we are in a better position to defend democracy against those who love it immoderately.

2

Beyond Nihilism:
Religion, Liberty, and the Art of Mediation

In decisive respects the West is a civilization shaped by its Christian inheritance. It owes to Christianity and the Christian spirit the separation of the things of Caesar and the things of God, the exalted place of conscience in its moral life, and its rejection of the monstrous and idolatrous Pharaonic state. But the West is much more than the "Old West," to adopt the revealing term of Danish historian David Gress. The "New West," the West that arose out of the Enlightenment, above all values science, technological progress, and human rights. It grows ever more estranged from its Christian and classical sources. We are confronted by this paradox: the "democratic revolution" of which Tocqueville was the prophet and diagnostician owes *something* to Christianity even as it erodes the Christian foundations of Western civilization.

At the same time, confronted by totalitarianism and other manifestations of modern nihilism, liberals and religious believers have found new reasons to see beyond past antagonisms. In his remarkable 1960 Eddington Lecture, "Beyond Nihilism," Michael Polanyi fully anticipated our situation. "The churches," he wrote, "seemed to recall modern man from a state beyond nihilism to his condition before the secular enlightenment." Yet modern man, democratic man, rightly rejects the authoritarian imposi-

tion of religion and does not wish "to go back on the scientific revolution which has secularized extensive domains of knowledge."
We do not wish to go back but we can no longer rest comfortably
with the modernist and postmodernist severing of truth and liberty, freedom and the moral contents of life. In this chapter, I will
explore the multiple dimensions of this problem with the help of
two contemporary students of the theological-political problem
in its Western form: the American political theorist Mark Lilla
and the French political philosopher Pierre Manent.

THE GREAT SEPARATION

If Pierre Manent insists that there can be no definitive solution to the theological-political problem, Mark Lilla calls for an
uncompromising return to the secularist foundations of modern liberal democracy. Lilla, a conservative turned demi-liberal,
is professor of the humanities at Columbia University and a
frequent contributor to the *New York Review of Books*. In *The
Stillborn God: Religion, Politics, and the Modern West* (2007), the
American political theorist highlights the various contemporary
threats to the "Great Separation" (I will follow him in capitaliz-
ing the phrase) between religion and politics that was theorized
by Thomas Hobbes in the seventeenth century and that, with
modifications, has became *the* basis of liberal constitutionalism
in the Western world.[1] For Lilla, the Great Separation is nothing less than the nonnegotiable foundation of modern liberty.
His book gives learned, eloquent expression to what one might
call *secular fundamentalism*—the belief that any public role for
religion or religious affirmation threatens human liberty as well
as the delicate "art of intellectual separation" at the heart of the
liberal order. By the latter phrase, Lilla means the separation of
politics and scientific inquiry from substantive ethical guidance,

from any comprehensive account of the good life for human beings.

One defect of Lilla's book is that it treats liberal or constitutional democracy almost exclusively as an epiphenomenal expression of the categories and assumptions of early modern political philosophy. Lilla shows no interest in specifically *religious* arguments for freedom of conscience and the separation of church and state. He also ignores the perspective of democratic statesmen who drew upon Christian as well as modern philosophical sources in articulating the rights and duties of men and citizens. For example, the American Declaration of Independence famously invokes both "nature's God" and God as "Creator," "Providence," and "Supreme Judge" of the world. It invokes "rights" but also speaks in a more traditional idiom of "prudence" and the requirements of personal and political "honor." With equal plausibility, it can be interpreted in light of modern deism and the "state of nature" doctrine of Hobbes and Locke *and* in light of an older tradition of natural law and natural right. To do full justice to the statesman's perspective would invariably lead one to question the simplistic identification of liberty with radical secularism and hence the self-evidence of the Great Separation in its most doctrinaire contemporary forms. Lilla is not prepared to take that risk. He thus forecloses all sorts of theoretical and practical possibilities. Still, he is not wrong to find in the political philosophy of Thomas Hobbes the most radical and self-conscious articulation of the Great Separation, an understanding that powerfully shaped more moderate articulations of the separation of church and state (such as John Locke's *A Letter Concerning Toleration*) and that has come to deeply influence the theory and practice of liberal constitutionalism.

Lilla is committed to a public sphere shorn of religion or any religiously inspired conceptions of the good life for human beings. He is a partisan, although a remarkably restrained one, of

what Richard John Neuhaus called "the naked public square"—
that is, a public realm devoid of any explicit religious symbolism
or affirmation. At the same time, he is sensitive to the historically exceptional and fragile character of the "liberal" separation
of religion and politics, power and opinion, truth and liberty.
He believes that a political-theological nexus that expressly con-
nects God, man, and the world better corresponds to the psychological needs and spiritual longings of human beings than the
austere secularism demanded by the modern liberal order. For
Lilla, the art of political and intellectual separation is a rare historical achievement that is vulnerable to criticism on philosophical, psychological, and political grounds. It has been subject to
legitimate criticism from philosophical critics such as Rousseau,
Kant, and nineteenth-century romantics who lamented its soul-
lessness—its heavy-handed abstraction from the spiritual and
poetic sides of our humanity. And it is under increasing assault
from the various fundamentalisms both in the West and in the
Islamic world that demand a restoration of political theology—
the full integration of religion and law—as the foundation of any
viable human order.

Why, then, have I called Lilla's approach an exercise in secularist fundamentalism? To begin with, Lilla shares no small
dose of the "anti-theological ire," as Leo Strauss called it, that
distorted the Enlightenment's purportedly rational approach to
the theological-political problem. His moderate tone, his seemingly measured cost-benefit analysis of the Great Separation,
coexists with and gives way to an illiberal demand for unending
vigilance against any political expression on the part of religious
believers. He seems to forget that believers have long made their
peace with liberal democracy (and in the American case played
a major role in establishing democratic institutions in the first
place). In addition, their publicly salutary insistence on justice
and personal responsibility is inseparable from certain religious

assumptions about man and the world. In this regard, Lilla is no less "authoritarian," no less committed to a rigorously naked public square, than more openly aggressive theorists of liberal "neutrality" such as John Rawls and Richard Rorty.

THE ARTS OF MEDIATION

As the political theorist Ralph C. Hancock has written in a particularly penetrating critique of *The Stillborn God*, Lilla has no room for "the arts of mediation," theoretical and practical efforts to think together or mediate the human and divine realms without conflating them or denying the legitimate (even precious) autonomy of the political sphere of human existence. Lilla makes only two references in his book to Alexis de Tocqueville, the modern student of democracy most committed to a "mediation" that would modify and humanize the separation of religion and liberty. At the heart of Tocqueville's intellectual and political project was an effort to promote the blending of the "spirit of liberty" and the "spirit of religion" in a way appropriate to a modern democratic age. He did so in full awareness of the dangers inherent in the old regime's conflation of religious and political authority. He supported the separation of church and state as something that was good for both politics and religion even as he emphasized the need for a robust if *indirect* role for religion in democratic public life. Lilla tersely rules out this project, arguing that "accommodation is not understanding." In response to this summary objection, Hancock raises the possibility of another approach that also surely deserves the appellation *liberal*:

> Might we propose renewing the project of understanding the accommodation and drawing upon concrete achievements of reconciling political and religious goods, not to solve the

27

problem but to refine and manage the claims of transcendence that must emerge in a substantially pluralistic society?

Despite his apparent evenhandedness in addressing the human consequences of the Great Separation, Lilla dogmatically eschews the path of mediation. His analysis is frozen in time: the one thing most needful is said to be a return to the Hobbesian roots of liberal democracy. Hobbes's *Leviathan*, appropriately "liberalized" by his great political and philosophical successors such as John Locke and David Hume, provides the core, nonnegotiable assumptions of Lilla's analysis of the relationship between religion and politics in the modern world. It is the true alternative to every form of romanticism, decisionism, and religious enthusiasm. For Lilla, religion almost always connotes messianic expectations as well as the negation of reason. Not that he wants to defend every aspect of Hobbes's thinking. Lilla freely concedes that the English philosopher takes atheism for granted, that he goes too far in reducing religion to a merely anthropological phenomenon, and that he unreasonably claims to have explained away the possibility of the self-revelation of a transcendent God. But such seemingly insuperable obstacles to taking Hobbes seriously as a guide to the religious question do not get in Lilla's way.

With Hobbes, we are called to accept the self-evidence of a "morally mute natural world" and to "separate our investigations of nature from our thoughts about God or the duties of man." Even if we have good reasons to quarrel *on rational grounds* with Hobbes's mechanistic and reductionist scientific "findings," Lilla argues, we may still profitably welcome his project. Not only has it liberated politics from ecclesiastical control but it has freed intellectual inquiry from the intrusions of theological and metaphysical reflection altogether. In Lilla's presentation, Hobbes's ferocious assault on "the vast Kingdom of Darkness" is the necessary precondition for the modern secular university, with its unending multiplication of autonomous disciplines and its rejection of any claim to unified truth about man or the whole. Hobbes may have been wrong in dogmatically reducing the sources of religious belief to nothing but superstition and fear, but Lilla does not hesitate to call the English political philosopher's position a "fortunate error." Lilla also claims, against the logic of his own position, that the Great Separation did not "presume or promote atheism." It is hard to reconcile a great crusade against the "Kingdom of Darkness" with more or less benign neutrality toward the private choice of religion within civil society. Is it plausible to suggest, as Lilla attempts to do, that Hobbes and other architects of the Great Separation "simply" taught that questions regarding "the basic structure of society" must be separated from "ultimate questions regarding God, the world, and human spiritual destiny"? Is this separation an end in itself or is it ultimately at the service of a more frontal assault on classical and Christian wisdom and the natural movement of the human soul toward the truth of things?

THE POLITICAL CONSEQUENCES OF HOBBES

Lilla presents a limited, one-sided picture of what Bertrand de Jouvenel called "the political consequences of Hobbes" in an important chapter in his 1955 masterwork *Sovereignty*. Jouvenel agrees with Leo Strauss and Michael Oakeshott that Hobbes is best understood as an individualist and liberal (or protoliberal) thinker and not, as is commonly claimed, as the father of modern totalitarianism. Hobbes's defense of "absolute" authority is at the service of securing the life and liberty of individuals and not of promoting a cult of state power. Leviathan, that "mortal god" among men, is conceived not on the model of a totalitarian state but rather as an instrument for stopping "the mischief which the intersection of [men's] appetites may do them." Hobbes's thought provides not only the theoretical inspiration for the radical separation of church and state but also the basic premises for modern political economy, that hedonistic "science" that identifies the goods of men with the things desired.

But if Hobbes's assumptions are indeed liberal, individualistic, and hedonistic, they are ultimately incompatible with self-government in both the moral (the government of the self) and political (civic self-rule) understandings of the term. With Hobbes, "absolute libertarianism" (the phrase is Jouvenel's) gives rise not only to hedonism and moral relativism but also to authoritarianism as a necessary means for maintaining the fragile social tie. A hedonistic society—a godless society—demands nothing less than a "strong and stable government." Jouvenel argues, convincingly in my view, that political liberty depends upon more elevated suppositions about human nature—and more noble and generous tendencies in the human soul—than those allowed in the official "system" of Hobbes. Beyond the neutral art or science of intellectual separation, Hobbes's political philosophy articulates and then builds upon a fearful and godless individualism. This individualism paradoxically has profoundly collectivist implications. Hobbes's philosophical and religious critics of old who derided "the monster of Malmsbury" in many cases had a deeper appreciation of the political consequences of his thought than the American political theorist fretting about the dangers posed by the "Christian Right" as he writes away in his study.

Lilla's selective appropriation of Hobbes is tied to a false dichotomy that structures his book as a whole. He repeatedly leaves his reader with a binary choice between "political theology" and the Great Separation. We are said to live "on the other shore" of that alternative since political theology is no longer a "living force"—a viable option—in our Western democratic societies. Lilla never comes to terms with the full implications of insisting, dogmatically I might add, that we modern liberal democrats conceive political life "solely with reference to man." He speaks of the need for human beings to take their bearings from this-worldly "lucidity" but never specifies what is the source of that alleged clarity. For Lilla, human self-sovereignty is a more or less benign affair that has nothing to do with the temptation for human beings to turn themselves into gods. Ignoring the critique of unmitigated human self-sovereignty that is common to both Christian and "conservative liberal" critics of radical modernity, he blames twentieth-century totalitarianism on theological "decisionism," (the view, as Lilla puts it, that there is "nothing rational, or even comprehensible, about God's decisions" and that man "must choose, for himself or for God, for history or for eternity") and continuing hopes for "religious apocalypse." At the same time, Lilla refuses to adequately acknowledge the link between totalitarianism and the atheistic fanaticism that denied all moral limits and culminated in the "self-enslavement" of man.

Lilla on the Totalitarian "Secular Religions"

When discussing the theological reflection of Karl Barth and Franz Rosenzweig, Lilla intimates that they are somehow indirectly responsible for the madness which was National Socialism. His account radically understates the anti-Christian character of National Socialism. He is, of course, on to something when he states that "eschatological language breeds eschatological politics no matter what dogmatic limits theologians try to place on it." The "analogical" approach of Catholic theology and its clear defense of the natural moral law avoided this danger to which certain currents of Protestant theology were prone. Remarkably, Lilla has *nothing* whatsoever to say about Catholic reflection on modernity because, he claims, the "institutional isolation of Catholic education" and the "Church's hostility to modern society" made it peripheral to the story he is telling. But the fact that a few students of Barth (though not Barth himself) succumbed to the delirium of National Socialism, and the philosopher Ernst Bloch combined "revolutionary Gnosticism" with support for East German totalitarianism, does not prove that transcendental religion was somehow the real source of the "impious cruelties" of the twentieth century. National Socialism was a brutal neopaganism that owed infinitely more to vulgar Nietzscheanism, half-baked "scientific racism," and Social Darwinism than to theological decisionism in any of its forms. Communism unleashed the most vicious assault on the Christian churches in human history. Both ideological movements denied common morality and a natural moral law—with murderous consequence—and sent many decent liberals back to the traditional moral sources of Western civilization (alas, some moved in the opposite direction and succumbed to the totalitarian temptation).

Moreover, religious conviction provided the strongest and most durable foundation for opposition to totalitarianism in the twentieth century, as the examples of Milosz, Kolakowski, John Paul II, and Solzhenitsyn amply attest. Lilla has written ably on totalitarianism in the past, particularly in his reflections on the "New French Thought," the non-Marxist and non-postmodernist currents that have come to the forefront in French political philosophy since the mid-1970s. But in this case his analysis is deformed by a poorly concealed antitheological ire. It is simply risible to argue, as Lilla does, that Hobbes provides the beginning of wisdom in confronting the phenomenon of "secular religion," of twentieth-century totalitarianism. Totalitarianism is not reducible to the category of religious "enthusiasm," as if the distinction between ersatz "secular religions" and authentic transcendental ones is finally a superficial one. As Michael Polanyi wrote in "Beyond Nihilism," "not all fanaticism is religious" in character. The morality of the totalitarians "was inverted and became immanent in brute force because a naturalistic view of man forced them into this manifestation. Once they are immanent, moral motives no longer speak in their own voice and are no longer accessible to moral arguments; such is the structure of moral nihilistic fanaticism."

MANENT ON THE THEOLOGICAL-POLITICAL PROBLEM IN ITS CHRISTIAN FORM

If Mark Lilla upholds a much too narrow and dogmatic conception of the Great Separation between religion and politics, his moderate tone concealing more radical and problematic assumptions, Pierre Manent's writings offer a rich, balanced, and suggestive rendering of the theological-political problem in its Western Christian form. Manent in no way disagrees with Lilla that the Great Separation forms the *starting point* for understanding liberty as liberty has been conceived and practiced for three centuries in the modern West. In fact, Manent argues that the Great Separation is the first and most fundamental of the multiple "separations" that together constitute the regime of modern liberty as a historically unique "organization of separations."[2] These include the separations between church and state, representatives and represented, and state and civil society, as well as the separation of powers within the constitutional order, the division of labor within the economic order, and the later conceptual distinction between "facts" and "values." The separation of "power" and "opinion" about the good life for human beings is at the heart of the self-consciously *modern*—and still enduring—"solution" to the theological-political problem.

But Manent appreciates, as Lilla does not, that the liberal West is the product of much more than the Great Separation. He *thinks* the accommodation that Ralph Hancock has so ably spoken of. A regime of consent depends upon a "body"—a political form such as the nation—that is an estimable inheritance from the West's predemocratic past. Western liberty in practice took shape from the fruitful coming together of the "neutral" liberal state and the *Christian* nation in a way that moderated the pretensions of early modern political philosophy to begin the world anew. For Manent, the great human and political imperative is to tie together "communion" and "liberty" in a way that does justice to both. The historical achievement of the democratic nation was inseparable from its capacity to do this. In contrast, philosophical liberalism has next to nothing to say about the necessity and desirability of the political art of weaving community and liberty together. It also regularly fails to consider the Christian religion on its own terms.

Christianity is a religion that in its dominant forms rejects theocracy and recognizes the autonomy of temporal authority within its own sphere. It accepts the legitimacy of the two cities, "the city of God" and the "city of man," and does not proclaim the need for a unitary law dictated by a mysterious, even capricious God. Unlike Lilla, Manent eschews all loose talk about "political theology," a category that derives from the apocalyptic musings of the right-wing jurist and social philosopher Carl Schmitt and that confuses more than it clarifies. Nature—the natural order of things—is the starting point, or at least *a* starting point, of distinctively Christian reflection about the good life and the proper ordering of the political community. But in a series of subtle analyses (see in particular the opening chapters of his *An Intellectual History of Liberalism*), Manent highlights the *structural* problem that the Christian Church posed for the integrity of the political order. Christianity left the temporal order free to organize itself as it would, but it reserved the right and duty of supervision. Faced with the millennial-old conflict between the rival claims of popes and emperors, ecclesiastical and temporal authority (as well as the competing spiritual claims made on behalf of biblical humility and pagan magnanimity), the capacious Christian synthesis of nature and grace began to fray.

The coup de grâce was the Reformation's sundering of the unity of Christendom and the ferocious wars of religion that ensued. Lilla writes as if the wars of religion were the ordinary and permanent political condition of the Christian world. Attempts to "solve" the European theological-political problem on the basis of a return to the political moderation of the classical philosophers were bound to fail because the basis of that political teaching was a doctrine of nature that could always be trumped—completed, perfected—by appeals to supernatural grace. But Hobbes's ferocious condemnation of the "Kingdom of Darkness" was much more than a repudiation of the political role of the Church. It was the rejection of the cosmological and moral assumptions underlying traditional philosophical and theological reflection and speculation.

Hobbes's polemical target was the intellectual and moral authority of Aristotle as it had been appropriated in the Christian West, "Aristotelity" as he wittily—and dismissively—called it in chapter 46 of *Leviathan*. The "natural philosophy" of the ancients was dismissed out of hand as a "dream" rather than true science, and their "moral philosophy" was said to tell us only about their own passions and nothing about what was intrinsically just and unjust, or good and evil. Hobbes denied any superintending principles above the human will, and located the source of the distinction between good and evil, and right and wrong, in the laws or conventions produced by the sovereign. He famously took his bearing not from what was good for human beings—and certainly not from some *summum bonum*—but from that ultimate evil, that *summum malum*—violent death—at the hands of others in the "state of nature" where the life of man is inevitably "solitary, nasty, brutish, and short." Despite the "geometric" or rationalist *form* of Hobbes's political science, he had no confidence whatsoever in the capacity of human reason to say *anything* about the substantial nature of man or the purposes of human freedom.

To be sure, Hobbes's architecture of separations played a crucial role in bringing civil peace to the West and in tracing the design of a *civil association* shorn of sectarian fanaticism. That is no mean achievement. As liberalized and democratized by his great successors such as Locke, Montesquieu, and Hume, the order of separations has allowed masses of human beings to live in relative peace and prosperity and has even found a real place for the goods of the soul—including religious freedom and affirmation—within civil society. But that is not the end of the story. Pierre Manent's work is particularly helpful in allowing us to see how the original separation must be mediated in practice and overcome in thought if the freedom and dignity of human beings is to be genuinely safeguarded.

As Manent writes in his 2006 book *La raison des nations: Réflexions sur la démocratie en Europe*, "If the separation of church and state is precious as a rule of our actions, it becomes ruinous if we make it the rule of our thought." To make it the rule of our thought is to deny the directedness of the human mind toward truth, toward "the sovereignty of the object." It is to permanently sever liberty from a searching engagement with the ends or purposes of human freedom. Lilla's "art of intellectual separation," in a desperate effort to maintain civil peace, risks giving rise to a new dogmatism that denies the natural movement of the human soul toward truth. It also assumes that the theological-political problem is frozen in time and ignores the new threats to human freedom that have arisen out of the modern "solution" to this

problem. Those threats include the specters of soft and hard despotism, as well as indifference to truth. These can be summed
up in the striking phrase of the Hungarian political philosopher
Aurel Kolnai: the "self-enslavement of man," which is a byproduct of the most radical and consistent interpretations of human
self-sovereignty.

BEYOND THE MODERN "SOLUTION"?

But to recognize the grave problems to which the modern "solution" to the West's theological-political problem has given rise
is not to gainsay the necessity of something like a "liberal" solution to the West's theological-political problem. There were good
reasons indeed for the "liberal" replacement of "authoritarian"
religion, "whose dogmas and commandments were a part of
political law," in Manent's words, by a radically new emphasis
on "rights" to freedom of religion or religious conscience. As
Manent writes in *The City of Man*, "The early Moderns separated
the law from the good because they had come to the conclusion
that it was no longer possible for the ends of man to have a place
in the law. Men had ideas about ends that were too incompatible;
these disagreements easily degenerated; what mattered above all
was to avoid civil war, which is the greatest of evils."

Some liberals also emphasized, in a manner not incompatible
with traditional moral philosophy, that truth and virtue must be
freely sought and chosen. Manent points out that liberal-minded
modern thinkers such as Milton (in his *Areopagitica*) and Less-
ing (in *The Education of the Human Race*) had high hopes that
the pursuit of truth and goodness would flourish when they were
freed from oppressive political and ecclesiastical control. There
was indeed something noble about the affirmation of liberty as
the essential precondition for the pursuit of virtue and truth and

the concomitant recognition that liberty itself must never lose sight of human excellence. Yet Manent is not being unduly negative when he suggests that these high hopes have been sorely disappointed. There is a need for new efforts at reviving these once noble liberal aspirations.

To be sure, the modern liberal order presupposes the "moral contents of life" and allows the citizen of liberal polities to practice his or her faith or pursue philosophical wisdom *privately*, within the realm of civil society. But as Marx argued in his 1844 essay "On the Jewish Question," "*presupposition* is the weakest form of affirmation." The goods of life have a necessarily tenuous or qualified status within the new liberal dispensation. They are not publicly recognized as goods (or such recognition is largely a residue of older religious and philosophical understandings) and this cannot help but diminish their significance to the modern "pursuit of happiness." One does not have to fully endorse Nietzsche's critique of liberal modernity as culminating in the victory of the "last man" who "invented happiness"—this being who lives only for the present moment and rejects all indebtedness to the past—to recognize the tensions between full-blown liberal relativism and a genuinely serious human life.

In *The City of Man*, Manent provides a particularly illuminating explanation for liberalism's drift toward militant indifference to truth. The *authorization* of every citizen to pursue his good in the private realm risks becoming a new command or injunction to ignore the pursuit of truth and goodness in the name of respecting the equality of every human being's subjective judgment. The liberal order allows indifference "toward all goods that are the object of human searching, even truth, which is the chief good." The spirit of radical modernity takes things a step further. The radical relativist *commands* indifference to the truth, thus giving rise to a new and paradoxical order of "authoritarian command," this time in the name of a punishing relativism or political correctness. What began as a salutary effort to prevent the appropriation of the idea of the good by political and ecclesiastical tyrants becomes a new source of tyranny and dehumanization, the "dictatorship of relativism" famously spoken of by Pope Benedict XVI a few days before his selection as pope in April 2005.

This analysis is in no way put forward with antiliberal intent. But the preservation of the noble aspirations of liberalism demands resisting the full implementation of the project of intellectual separation, since that project ultimately demands the radical severing of human freedom from the moral contents of life. The law cannot be fully "neutral" about the good life— about the ends and purposes of human life—without eventually subverting the idea of human nobility and the moral foundations of liberty itself.

THE EMANCIPATION OF THE WILL

In a remarkably synthetic 1993 essay entitled "Christianity and Democracy: Some Remarks on the Political History of Religion, or, on the Religious History of Modern Politics," Manent brilliantly highlights the dialectical twists and turns that have defined the relationship between religion and politics under conditions of modernity. In important respects, he argues, modernity can be understood as a self-conscious project committed to the "emancipation of the will" from any subordination to the dual requirements of nature and grace. This emancipation finds its most willful expressions in the theoretical and practical radicalism of Machiavelli and Nietzsche, two thinkers at the beginning and end of the modern movement who combined "the unlimited affirmation of the human will" with an "unlimited polemic against Christianity." Still, the success of our democracies serves to obscure "the extraordinary audacity of the original project of establishing the human world on the narrow point of the human will."

Manent points out that it was the Catholic Church that for the longest time insisted that liberalism (or naturalism, as it sometimes called it) would inevitably give way to more radical and consistent forms of human self-affirmation such as socialism or communism. It is easy today to criticize the Church for its failure to appreciate the considerable benefits of the new liberal order. But for all its faults, the Church was properly sensitive to the "willfulness" inherent in the modern project. It was not wrong to discern totalitarian tendencies at work in modern democracy. As Manent points out, it was the experience of "totalitarian democracy" in both its Jacobin and Bolshevik forms that led to a specifically *liberal* discovery—or rediscovery—of religion and to a more robust Christian or Catholic defense of constitutionalism and human rights. Conservative-minded liberals and anti-totalitarian Christians were henceforth united by a rejection of human self-sovereignty. They came to appreciate that the "regulated will," one that deferred to God and the law, and not one emancipated from natural and moral restraints, is the hallmark of a genuinely free and humane social order.

CONSTANT AND TOCQUEVILLE: THE LIBERAL REDISCOVERY OF RELIGION

Manent cites Benjamin Constant as an exemplar of this paradoxical reconciliation between Christianity and liberalism. The Swiss-born Constant was a Huguenot and anticleric who had no sympathies for the old regime or the political power of the Catholic Church. Yet he was appalled by the antireligious terrorism that accompanied the French Revolution and defended the rights and integrity of ordinary Catholic believers. Moreover, he saw in the terrible work of the French Revolutionary Convention the *effectual truth* of modern doctrines of sovereignty—the terror that flowed from making willfulness, no matter where it originated, whether from the one, the few, or the many—the foundation of collective life. As Constant famously put it in the opening chapter of *Principles of Politics Applicable to All Governments* (1815), "There are things too heavy for human hands."

Constant did not abandon the idea of the general will altogether, since, properly interpreted, it was a way of combining majority rule with good government and the common good. But he rejected the "false metaphysics" that confused human liberty with the unfettered will of the people. In his political writings, he took aim at the confusion of the popular sources of authority with a guarantee of justice and the general good. He set out to rescue liberalism from that revolutionary inebriation that refused to bow before sacred limits or restraints. He never stopped repeating that "there is a part of human existence which remains individual and independent, and by right beyond all political jurisdiction." Confronting the first manifestations of totalitarian democracy, Constant broke with the official ideology of the French Revolution and affirmed that "sovereignty exists only in a limited or relative way."

Like Burke or the French counterrevolutionaries such as Joseph de Maistre, Constant criticized the pretensions of modern philosophy and affirmed a spiritual realm or space above the human will. Unlike the conservative or reactionary critics of the French Revolution, however, he used this insight at the service of a chastened liberalism. However, one must note that he never defines the ultimate source of these limits upon the human will. He evokes religion as a reminder of the sublime and a symbol of the ineffable, as the source of generous feelings and noble action, and as a consolation amidst misery. He sympathized with religion without being particularly religious and had none of Tocqueville's (qualified) sympathies for traditional faith. He is finally clearer about what he rejects—absolute sovereignty or unlimited willfulness—than he is about what he affirms. Constant is the first modern thinker to limn a "negative" argument for an order of things above the human will. Like many twentieth-century antitotalitarian thinkers, he is too much of a modern man to simply believe in the old verities and far too decent—and reflective—to dispense with them altogether.

As Manent argues, conservative-minded liberals such as Constant and Tocqueville found for religion "its specifically modern moral political and moral credibility." They praised it "for the very reason it was formerly and even recently criticized: it is something *above* the human will." Constant saw that religion kept human beings in mind of the noble and the beautiful, and of those obligations that transcend the will of men. For his part, Tocqueville deplored a "pantheism" that conflated the divine and human and that weakened moral agency by making human beings playthings of vast cosmological, historical, and sociological forces. He, too, deplored absolute and unlimited human sovereignty and attacked the "impious maxim" that "in the interest of society all is permitted." For Tocqueville, Manent notes, religion could moderate the effects of both the "new activism" and the "new passivity" to which democracy gave rise. As Tocqueville famously argues in the opening chapters of the second volume of *Democracy in America*, democratic theorists proclaim that human beings should take their bearings only from their own lights, that they should disregard the authority of tradition or anything that is not discernable by the light of reason. But human beings need authoritative beliefs or "dogmas" to live well. Without the moral maxims provided by religion they are likely to succumb to a psychological and spiritual "vertigo" that gives way either to nihilism or to conformism with all its illiberal political consequences.

The conclusion is clear: liberty must be "liberty under God" if it is to do justice to the spiritual nature and limitations of human beings. Liberty understood as pure indetermination does not allow human beings to avoid the twin temptations of democratic tyranny and the listlessness born of exaggerating our capacity to make our way in the world unguided by the spiritual or philosophical inheritance of the past. And listlessness leads to despotism. Of such thoughts, Lilla seems to have no inkling.

FROM SELF-SOVEREIGNTY TO SELF-ENSLAVEMENT

The Communist revolution of the twentieth century gave further impetus to the reconciliation between conservative liberalism and Christian constitutionalism. Thinkers such as Bertrand de Jouvenel, Aurel Kolnai, and the ex-Marxist Polish philosopher Leszek Kolakowski have highlighted the multiple ways in which the "self-deification" of man inevitably leads to his "self-enslavement." A liberal order depends upon modesty, a sense of limits, and opposition to any and all efforts to make idols of a class or race, or to imbue the Historical Process with pseudosacred significance. Totalitarian collectivism denied the primordial distinction between good and evil and replaced it with an ungrounded distinction between progress and reaction. In light of this mutilation of the moral life of men, liberals rediscovered the dependence of liberty upon conceptions of natural and divine justice that are required to temper human willfulness and which provide an intellectual context for moral conscience. In his classic 1945 work *On Power*, Jouvenel remarked on the tendency of law in the contemporary world to become "ambulatory," or disconnected from unchanging or eternal verities, when sovereignty—human power—is treated as an end in itself. The illiberal, even totalitarian consequences of this movement are clear enough. Even more profoundly, totalitarianism, especially in its Communist forms, revealed the collectivist logic inherent in secular humanitarianism. A political order that respects human dignity conceives of human beings as "participants" in an order they did not make and cannot ultimately control. But absolute notions of sovereignty lead not only to tyranny but also to "pantheistic" or "identitarian" conceptions of human equality that tend to swallow up genuine human individuality. Shorn of a grounding in natural right and a metaphysics of participation, egalitarianism points toward a dehumanizing centralization and uniformity.

In his 1949 essay "Privilege and Liberty," Aurel Kolnai brilliantly traces the tendency of atheistic humanitarianism to devolve into an "identitarian" or "collectivist" insistence on "oneness of mind" and "uniformity of type." He locates this tendency in the "indetermination" of its concept of the "common good." Since there is "no Entity and no Law *above* man, no definite and subsistent good outside man to measure and to direct his corporate action," there is an inexorable tendency to judge what is good or obligatory by what is "self-evident" to everybody and anybody. "Human subjectivity" becomes the judge of truth. As a result, moral anarchy can be avoided only by "the actual sameness and fusion of human thoughts and volitions as such." The faux unity put forward by secular totalitarianism replaces the quest to discern a transcendent cause, measure, and end behind the flux of things. Participation in "an order of things" is replaced with the collective worship of a unitary human subjectivity. This is, of course, only one outcome of secular humanitarianism. But it is a "logical" outcome and one that gives rise to a tyranny that makes the tyrannies of old look both benign and self-limiting. When Solzhenitsyn stated, as he did in his 1983 Templeton Lecture, that totalitarianism arose in no small part because "men had forgotten God," he was making a philosophical claim and not merely one rooted in faith or piety.

Raymond Aron was not a religious believer, at least in any conventional sense. But he often said that he was horrified by the "idolatrous" character of the "secular religions," their disregard of common morality and their rejection of transcendent principles, of a "space" above the human will. In arguably his deepest treatment of this question, the 1956 essay "Fanaticism, Prudence, and Faith," he argued that ideological fanaticism had its ultimate root in radical skepticism—nihilism—about the first principles of human thought and action. He was angered and perplexed by the indulgence shown toward Communism by "fellow-traveling" existentialist philosophers such as Sartre and by progressivist Christians. The former denied "any permanence to human nature" and "oscillate[d] between a lawless voluntarism and a doctrinairism based on myths." The progressivist Christians succumbed to the "idolatry of History" and ignored the savage persecution of believers under "really-existing socialism."

In the magisterial conclusion of his 1956 essay, Aron writes,

> For want of principles both existentialists and progressivist Christians count on a class or historical dialectic to provide them with conviction. Dogmatic when they should be prudent, the existentialists have begun by denying what they should have affirmed. They have no use for prudence, "the god of this world below" (Burke); they invest the historical movement with reason after having divested it of man. The progressivists attribute to Revolution that sacred quality which they are afraid of no longer finding in the life of the Church and the adventure of souls.

Aron directed his own critical skepticism, then, not at "authentic faith" but at abstract "schemes, models, and utopias." Aron ended his essay by stating that he had "less against fanaticism" than "against nihilism, which is its ultimate origin."

If Kolnai's or Jouvenel's analyses point toward a more conservative or traditional understanding of the foundations of human liberty, Aron renews the Constantian appreciation of religion and the moral law on liberal and philosophical grounds. Despite the differences that separate these approaches, both emphatically repudiate the ideological distortion of reality and of human freedom. In their distinct ways they point to the inadequacy of identifying human liberty with modern willfulness and with a dogmatic atheism, scientism, and humanitarianism that denies the spiritual nature and moral responsibilities of human beings. Of course, all of these can be found in Hobbes.

THE CHURCH AND LIBERAL DEMOCRACY: WHAT KIND OF ACCOMMODATION?

Our analysis has stressed the vulnerability of philosophical liberalism to subversion from within. Various forms of "hard" and "soft" self-sovereignty (I owe this helpful distinction to Jean Bethke Elshtain[3]) threaten to erode the moral foundations of democracy. If the temptation of a certain kind of decayed liberalism is to identify "choice" or "consent" with willful self-assertion (in the seemingly more liberal and benign form of support for abortion on demand, cloning, and various forms of biotechnological "enhancement"), the temptation of conservatives (or conservative-minded liberals) is to think that the problem that self-sovereignty poses for modern democracy can be rhetorically defined out of existence. For the conservative-minded, this takes the form of "baptizing" liberal democracy in a way that obscures its connections to the modern Enlightenment project. This is the temptation that the post–Vatican II Catholic Church has not always successfully resisted.

A series of prominent twentieth-century Catholic thinkers from the French Thomist philosopher Jacques Maritain to Pope

John Paul II have located the origins of equality and the "rights of man" in the teachings of the Gospels themselves. They have been too eager to argue for the *essential* compatibility of Christianity and democracy rather than putting the stress on the need for a prudential accommodation between the Church and the liberal order. For all its practical merits, this Christian democratic position obscures the origins of philosophical liberalism in a polemical reaction to the political power of the Church. It also ignores the insight of an older, more antimodern Church that the rights of man were too often claimed at the expense of the rights of God.

Instead of proclaiming the Christian origins of liberalism, or confusing Christianity with secular humanitarianism, as progressivist Christians are prone to do, the Church can contribute to the cause of freedom by upholding the truth as it understands it. When Pope Benedict XVI warned in his September 2006 Regensburg Address against reducing Christianity to a "humanitarian moral message," he was speaking both in the name of the integrity of the faith and out of genuine solicitude for the well-being of a liberal or democratic order. Christianity can exercise its influence on the souls of men, it can help fortify an understanding of liberty as "liberty under God," only if it rejects the temptation to become a wholly "democratic" religion. The Church does not serve the cause of human liberty, it cannot play its part in overcoming the democratic "activism" and "passivity" so feared by Tocqueville, unless it stands for something more substantial than a commitment to humanitarian "values" and egalitarian "social justice."

Nor do persistent demands for the internal "democratization" of the churches contribute to their ability to remind democratic men and women of the ultimate dependence of liberty upon truth. The churches would then bow to consent as their governing principle. We have arrived at what we might call the Tocquevillian conundrum or problematic: liberal democracy needs the wisdom, self-restraint, and elevation provided by religion, but over time democracy tends to democratize all the contents of life, including religion itself. As thinly disguised humanitarianism, as a project to promote this-worldly transformation, religion ceases to be "something *above* the human will."

TOWARD A CHASTENED LIBERALISM

Careful reflection on this problem serves to moderate any excessive hopes for creating a new postliberal consensus that could purge liberalism of its intrinsic—and historical—identification with human self-sovereignty. The nineteenth-century American Catholic journalist, writer, and political philosopher Orestes Brownson perfectly captured the nature of this conundrum in his 1865 work *The American Republic*. Brownson noted that the "state of nature" doctrine—the idea that government arises from a compact or contract among equal, independent, and sovereign individuals—was part of the "political tradition" of the United States. In the famous words of the Declaration of Independence, government "derives its just powers from the consent of the governed." All Americans—one might add almost everyone in the liberal West today—agree that no man has the right to govern another human being without his consent. But some locate this prohibition against despotic rule in the absolute freedom or "autonomy" of the individual, while others, including many of the founders themselves, denied that the individual has a "sovereign right even to himself, or the right to dispose of himself as he pleases," notes Brownson. The state of nature doctrine is thus remarkably equivocal: it can be understood in light of the requirements of either autonomy or a more traditional understanding of "liberty under God." In this equivocation or indetermination one can find the deepest roots of the "culture wars" that have raged in the United States (and to some extent in other Western democracies) in recent decades.

We are left with a choice: we can conceive Man as sovereign lord of existence, the autonomous creator of his own "values," or we can see in him a being who participates in a natural order that he did not make, an "order of things" that gives meaning to his freedom and that makes sense of his search for truth. In the latter understanding, eloquently upheld by Brownson, "man is not God, independent, self-existing, and self-sufficing." Rather, "he is dependent, and dependent not only on his Maker, but on his fellow-men, on society, and even on nature, or the material world." The task of a chastened liberalism, no less than of a Christian religion faithful to its own wisdom, is to remind men and women inebriated with the ideology of consent that human beings are truly free only when they know they are not gods. The next task is to draw the appropriate moral and political conclusions from this insight.

Part II

Statesmanship in an Egalitarian Age

3

Taking Greatness Seriously:
Statesmanship in a Democratic Age

The study of statesmanship, of excellence in its various political manifestations, is particularly necessary—and salutary—in a democratic age. It punctures our egalitarian illusions and reminds us of those rare human qualities—courage, moderation, foresight, prudence, and magnanimity, among them—that are worthy of admiration in every time and place. These qualities not only are admirable in themselves but are also necessary for sustaining free political communities, especially in times of crisis. The twentieth century was deformed by the ubiquitous cult of the Leader—the *Führer, Duce*, or *Vozhd*—shorn of any concern for the moral law and the qualities of soul that are integral to true human greatness. Yet our social science, committed to the radical heterogeneity of facts and values, is preoccupied with "charismatic leadership" conceived in a morally neutral way. Washington and Churchill, at one extreme, and Hitler and Stalin, at the other, are placed in the same analytic basket in a manner that effaces the crucial difference between the authentic statesman and the demagogue or ideological tyrant.

It is thus particularly difficult to take greatness seriously today. In addition to the aforementioned intellectual confusions, "elitism" in all its forms is the bête noire of advanced intellectual circles. When academics and intellectuals do turn to the study of great men and great texts, it is too often with subversive intent, with the express purpose of denying their greatness.

But there have been important exceptions. The distinguished émigré political philosopher Leo Strauss, who did so much to revive classical political science in our time, spoke eloquently about the contributions that a true study of politics could make in spontaneous remarks that he delivered in class at the University of Chicago on January 25, 1965. The occasion was the death of Winston Churchill. The academic study of politics, he suggested, had a highest duty: "To remind ourselves and our students, of political greatness, human greatness, of the peaks of human excellence." The task of a genuine science of society is to see things as they are, "and this means above all in their greatness and misery, their excellence and their vileness, their nobility and their triumphs." In doing so, we train ourselves and our students "never to mistake mediocrity, however brilliant, for true greatness."

Strauss captured an essential aspect of the "scientific" study of society all but ignored by its contemporary practitioners: to understand human reality adequately, objectively, we must make the effort to understand the full range of human motives and achievements. We must make every effort to describe and understand those rare peaks of political life, which put the ordinary and prosaic in their proper perspective. An appreciation of true human greatness does not make us despise the run-of-the-mill, but it does allow us to see its limits. The statesmanship of Washington, Lincoln, Churchill, or de Gaulle, for example, can never be adequately understood if they are subsumed under a general theory of leadership or are reduced to the category of "power" as some generalized motive of political life.

THE OBSTACLES TO POLITICAL UNDERSTANDING

In a truly open-minded consideration, the phenomena must be allowed to reveal themselves without the distortion of historical or sociological reductionism. But the obstacles to understanding political things in their manifold "greatness and misery" are greater than we might expect. It is no easy task to become naïve again. Modern theory and practice place seemingly insuperable obstacles in the way of an authentic appreciation of political life.

Tocqueville is an extremely helpful guide on this score because he helps diagnose the maladies and prescribe certain remedies. He famously warned about the tendency of democratic intellectual life to homogenize reality, to ignore those qualitative distinctions that constitute reality. In Tocqueville's view, the study of political greatness is a salutary antidote to this tendency, so evident in the contemporary intellectual's scorn for "elitism."

Tocqueville provides further insight into the neglect of human greatness in a democratic age. In a particularly striking chapter at the beginning of volume 2 of *Democracy in America*, Tocqueville suggests that democratic historians privilege great "general causes" over the influence of particular individuals in their interpretation of modern society. This emphasis, however, is not simply arbitrary—there is indeed a diminished role for human agency in modern democratic societies. We are all familiar with the abstractions—democratization, industrialization, urbanization, modernization, and globalization—that dominate contemporary political discourse. These abstractions refer to real phenomena that shape and limit political choice. We are not free to ignore them. Tocqueville himself did not hesitate to resort to such "general causes" when attempting to make sense of the emerging democratic order. He appreciated that "general facts explain more things in democratic centuries than in aristocratic centuries, and particular influences fewer." But he insisted that the virtues and vices of a few still have the power to shape the destiny of peoples. Political communities are not merely subject to what Tocqueville called "inflexible providence or to a blind fatality."

Raymond Aron updated Tocqueville's analysis in light of the intellectual dominance of Marxism, as well as various reductive currents of social science in the twentieth century. In a 1960 essay entitled "The Dawn of Universal History," Aron argued that sociological "doctrinaires" such as Marx and Comte taught much that is valuable concerning the "historical mutation"—capitalism, industrial society, modern technological science—transforming the modern world. But they mistakenly "argued as if history, in the sense of the succession of wars and empires, of victories and defeats, was over and done with." They "underestimate[d] the durability of the traditional aspect of history—the rise and fall of empires, the rivalry between regimes, the beneficial or baleful exploits of great men." Aron therefore called for a new way of thinking that could do justice to both "drama" and "process," "history as usual" and "the originality of industrial society." The task of the modern student of politics and history is daunting: it is nothing less than to analyze "the dialectical interpenetration" of traditional history, with its rivalry of regimes, and the distinctive general causes that are in the process of transforming modern life and that often seem to escape human control.

The Study of Statesmanship

We have considered some of the obstacles to a recovery of a true political science as well as the new circumstances within which such a political science must operate. The study of the thought

56

and action of outstanding statesmen is central to political science rightly understood and is a crucial means for rekindling an appreciation of human greatness amidst the leveling tendencies of a democratic age. I insist: we must study the *thought* as well as the action of great statesmen. Now, it is true that reading the biographies of such statesmen is popular among part of the reading public today. This habit is to be commended. But one must add two cautionary notes: most biographers at best pay lip service to the writings of great statesmen; and much historical writing is too distorted by either a narrow sense of "objectivity" or egalitarian resentment against the category of greatness to do full justice to the greatness of extraordinary statesmen. I believe that we finally must turn to the speeches and writings of great statesmen themselves. To be sure, the writings of such men should be approached critically, but also with a receptivity that enables us to learn from their examples and insights.

Let us turn to the two great European statesmen who navigated their countries through the storms of the Second World War. Winston Churchill and Charles de Gaulle not only embodied greatness but also thought rigorously about its character, its permanent preconditions, and the specific threats to it in a modern egalitarian age. In their greatness, Churchill and de Gaulle were also friends of democratic liberty. They were democracy's friends, precisely because they were willing to confront its limitations, and to do what is possible to address them within the bounds of prudence and decency. One avenue was through great rhetoric. Their sometimes grandiose rhetoric was a reminder that humans remain "political animals" even in a democratic age. Despite their attachment to human excellence, neither Churchill nor de Gaulle ever doubted the fundamental justice of our democratic regimes.

Yet these antitotalitarian statesmen were far from simpleminded democrats. They were too aware of other human possibilities to limit their horizons to democratic modernity. They also had a penetrating grasp of democratic modernity's deepest characteristics. De Gaulle believed that totalitarianism was an episode in a more fundamental "crisis of civilization" tied to the rise of mass society and the erosion of traditional moral, political, and spiritual authority. This deepest of modern statesmen meditated on the political consequences of the "death of god." His most thoughtful reflection on the crisis of modern mass society and the threats to human dignity that accompany the unfolding of modernity can be found in his speech at Oxford University on November 25, 1941. I have analyzed that speech at some length in *De Gaulle: Statesmanship, Grandeur, and Modern Democracy* (2000). Here, I would like to discuss an equally remarkable text of Churchill called "Mass Effects in Modern Life." This text was written in 1925 and published in *Thoughts and Adventures* in 1932. It is a profound meditation on the possibilities and prospects for human greatness in an egalitarian age.

"MASS EFFECTS IN MODERN LIFE"

"Mass Effects in Modern Life" explores the relative weight of "drama" and "process" in human affairs, to employ the helpful formulation of Raymond Aron. A cursory survey of history, Churchill observes, indicates "the decisive part which accident and choice play at every moment." Even more formative is the influence of "Master Teachers—Thinkers, Discoverers, Commanders" who have left their mark on history at every turn. But, in a manner reminiscent of both Tocqueville and Aron, Churchill asks if the destiny of mankind is not "already escaping from the control of individuals. Are not our affairs increasingly being settled by mass processes?" Does modernity entail a new situation where human agency is no longer the decisive element shaping individual or collective destinies?

In the contemporary world one observes a marked decline in personal eminence. The "Great Contemporaries" that so impressed Churchill in his book of that name (1937) were for the most part Victorian statesmen and gentlemen, figures who already seemed to belong to the very distant past. In the intellectual, cultural, and political realms, "vacant thrones" abound. Humankind advances to new heights, but individual men are in seemingly permanent eclipse.

Churchill saw "enormous processes of collectivization" at work everywhere in modern societies. In some cases these processes, such as economic mass production, contributed mightily to the progress and prosperity of society. But despite its palpable economic benefits, such collectivization left a much more questionable impact on the "character and psychology" of men and societies. Our modern societies were succeeding in providing a "measureless abundance" unthinkable to previous ages. But this came at the expense of personal initiative and civic independence.

In modern mass society, public opinion is largely prepackaged, shaped by a media that supplies the populace with "a continuous stream of standardized opinion." Education is "at once universal and superficial," producing "standardized citizens all engulfed with regulation opinions, prejudices and sentiments."* Modern mass society may "eventually lead to a reasonable, urbane and highly serviceable society." But Churchill adds a cautionary note: these mass effects may well be "destructive of those conditions of personal stress and mental effort to which the masterpieces

---

* The rise of the Internet and the proliferation of new media do not *fundamentally* alter the broad processes of "standardization" at work in the contemporary world. The cacophony of voices that one encounters on the Internet coexist with a remarkable standardization of rhetoric and perspectives that is characteristic of a democratic age. But it is nonetheless the case that the new technologies make it more difficult than ever for the state to monopolize communications and thus to impose "totalitarian" uniformity on civil society.

of the human mind are due." Churchill suggests that democratic justice comes at the expense of human greatness, even as an aristocratic order that gave rise to Master Teachers and to genuine masterpieces of the human mind paid insufficient attention to the dignity of the common man.

Thankfully, Churchill notes, there are limits to the standardization of human beings. These limits are indicated by the "universal standardization" which was the aim of Soviet Bolshevism. The Bolsheviks attempted by "tyranny and by terror to establish the most complete form of mass life and collectivism of which history bears record." Writing in 1925, Churchill argued that such a totalitarian enterprise was bound to fail. "Human nature is more intractable than ant-nature," he wisely insisted.

Advanced liberal societies can take comfort that they have escaped the clutches of totalitarianism. Still, "the great emancipated nations seem to have become largely independent of famous guides and guardians." The Hero, Commander, or Teacher is largely a residue of "bygone rugged ages." Technologically driven modern warfare apparently doesn't need them, and standardized opinion seems to make their insights obsolete. Yet Churchill sensed a profound "restlessness" at work among his contemporaries. Modern men "miss [their] giants." Churchill cannot help wondering whether a world of mass effects is humanly satisfying. He writes:

> Can modern communities do without great men? Can they dispense with hero-worship? Can they provide a larger wisdom, a nobler sentiment, a more vigorous action, by collective processes, than were ever got from the Titans? Can nations remain healthy, can all nations draw together, in a world whose brightest stars are film stars and whose gods are sitting in the gallery? Can the spirit of man emit the vital spark by machinery? Will the new problems of successive

generations be solved successfully by "the common sense of most," by party caucuses, by Assemblies whose babble is no longer heeded? Or will there be some big hitch in the forward march of mankind, some intolerable block in the traffic, some vain wandering into the wilderness; and will not then the need for a personal chief become the mass desire?

The conclusion to "Mass Effects on Modern Life" is equivocal. Churchill suggests that nature abhors a vacuum, and that the spirit of man must find higher satisfactions than those offered in a standardized world. Yet he somberly warns against the cult of the leader and suggests "we must take the loss with the gain. On the uplands there are no fine peaks." We must resign ourselves, then, for the most part to a kind of decent mediocrity. But this is not the whole story. The citizens of liberal communities can take pride in the freedom and initiative that nonetheless persist in such societies.

But Churchill's own deeds are assuredly his final word. As a citizen, Churchill willingly accepted the priority of justice to greatness. But he knew full well that our uplands must occasionally aspire to more than mediocrity and mass effects. Sometimes it is forced upon them. Without this aspiration, democracy loses its capacity to speak to or to inspire the highest capacities of our nature. It may be that it takes a profound crisis—something on the order of 1861 or 1940 or even the events of September 11, 2001—to arouse democratic individuals from their slumbers. But as long as chance reigns, the order of democratic justice will need greatness to sustain itself. Such greatness is also a salutary reminder of the full range of human possibilities. The study of the thought and action of statesmen such as Lincoln, Churchill, and de Gaulle is crucial to the civic and moral health of democratic peoples. It is also necessary for understanding the heights that politics, even democratic politics, may in principle attain.

At the same time, one must add, it is necessary to be sensitive to the dangers posed by demagogic appeals to charismatic leadership. One must never lose sight of the fact that constitutionalism and the rule of law remain the indispensable foundations, the pediment (as the political theorist Thomas L. Pangle has put it), of a free and civilized political order.

ADDENDUM: TRUE AND FALSE GREATNESS

I have suggested that many influential academic historians and political theorists are partisans of "democratic history" in the sense defined by Tocqueville: they are suspicious of anything that smacks of "elitism" and downplay or even deride the role of great men in shaping the course of history. Paul Johnson's *Heroes: From Alexander the Great and Julius Caesar to Churchill and de Gaulle* (2007) is a notable exception. It is a brilliant, if flawed, investigation of the ambiguities inherent in human greatness. The book's subtitle only begins to convey the impressive range that it covers.

Johnson's subjects run the gamut from warrior-kings and conquerors such as Alexander the Great and Julius Caesar—who inhabit the thin line between the heroic and the reckless, between superhuman courage and monstrous killing for its own sake—to biblical heroes and heroines such as Deborah, Samson, and David, who put guile, might, and deception at the service of justice and God's beleaguered people. Johnson especially appreciates "exemplary heroes" such as Henry V and Joan of Arc, who combined the Christian and martial virtues and never lost sight of the requirements of the common good. He also holds in high regard military men such as Washington, Nelson, and Wellington, who inspired their soldiers' admiration while resisting the "Napoleonic" temptation to make them cannon fodder for personal ambition or military or ideological despotism. Johnson relates these heroes' stories with an eye for the telling detail and the memorable *bon mot*.

Johnson artfully conveys the superhuman virtuosity of Alexander and Caesar, even as he chronicles Caesar's unconscionably bloody deeds in Gaul and Alexander's slow descent into the cruelties and excesses of what used to be called "oriental despotism." He writes with admiration for biblical heroines, whose deeds reveal the limitations of a heroism reduced to brute force and shorn of poetry, beauty, and guile. The biblical Jews, Johnson writes in a striking formulation, "were weak in the physics of survival, strong in the metaphysics." He admires medieval kingship at its best, even as he traces a "daunting necrology" of British kings who died in battle, or from disease or gastric ailments, or cruelly at the hands of rivals.

Johnson's hatred for Napoleon is palpable, as is his admiration for Washington's self-restraint and Lincoln's inimitable combination of nobility, justice, and prudent ambition. Johnson shows that the careers of great human beings can "evoke wonder or admiration or respect or in some cases sympathy," while at the same time being morally ambiguous and in some cases even monstrous. Such is surely the case with Alexander and Caesar but also—to a lesser extent, of course—with the majority of heroic men throughout human history. While far from a pacifist, Johnson, like his great predecessor Samuel Johnson, has no sympathy for "heroes" who are little more than killing machines.

Rare indeed is the Cincinnatus or Washington whose ambition is noble enough to know when to go home, or the Lincoln "who has brooded so long on the nature of political truth and justice, and the frailty of man in promoting them" that he can stir men to action and reflection through wise and poetic utterances that "cling to the memory," such as the Gettysburg Address and the Second Inaugural Address. To the rank of those both great and

good, Johnson gives pride of place to the sixteenth-century English statesman Thomas More. He admires More as a statesman,
hero, and martyr because of his rare nobility in both life and
death. No stranger to the ways of the world, More knew the difference between a king and tyrant, as his unfinished biography of
Richard III made clear. Portraying a king who became, in Johnson's words, a "tyrant and a devouring wolf" who imperiled the
bodies and souls of men, More's study also served, in Johnson's
estimation, as "a theoretical preparation, a dress rehearsal for his
own conflict with Henry VIII." More died in a dignified way, in
defense of an ideal of Christian kingship unsullied by the lawlessness of the tyrant. Given his admiration for More's thought
and statesmanship, it is perplexing that Johnson confuses More's
Utopia with a blueprint for "ideological" despotism in the modern sense. As the best scholars have established, More's book is by
contrast a work in the tradition of classical political philosophy:
the "ideal society" that transcends conflict, division, and human
passion is literally *ou topos*, no-place.

GETTING CHURCHILL AND DE GAULLE RIGHT

Johnson's chapter on Churchill and de Gaulle ("A Generous Hero
and a Heroic Monster") should have been one of the book's highlights. Unfortunately, Johnson provides no analysis of Churchill's
great wartime speeches or of his deeply insightful books on politics and history, though he does have some interesting things to
say about his subject's heroic and generous character, his surpris-
ingly superficial views about religion (he was a pagan through
and through), and his deep-seated *pietás* toward British history
and constitutional institutions.*

---

* Johnson goes some way toward redressing this lacuna in his lucid and insightful biographical essay *Churchill* (New York: Viking, 2009), which builds upon

64

His treatment of de Gaulle is even less satisfactory. Johnson appreciates that de Gaulle is a great statesman who twice saved his beloved France from defeat and disgrace—in 1940 and again in 1958. He acknowledges that de Gaulle's "transcendental gift of reflecting upon the process of history" has much to teach us. Yet while Johnson never confuses this "authoritative" man with a political authoritarian or an aspiring tyrant, he makes outlandish judgments about "chronic halitosis" being the source of de Gaulle's personal austerity and aloofness. His sole source for this claim, Malcolm Muggeridge, notes in his memoir *Chronicles of Wasted Time* only that in his own experience, a de Gaulle fresh off the battlefield, with ruffled hair and slightly bad breath, still came across as an authentic hero.

Johnson calls de Gaulle an inhuman "monster," bereft of warmth and affection. He never mentions the French statesman's tender relations with his mentally retarded daughter Anne, who died at the age of twenty in 1948. He brands de Gaulle an "intellectual" who ultimately put ideas above people (the ultimate Johnsonian insult). He never comes to terms with de Gaulle's severe criticisms of Napoleon for divorcing "grandeur" and moderation, or his condemnation of the military and political elites

---

his more impressionistic treatment of the English statesman in *Heroes* while introducing some new themes and emphases. In *Churchill*, Johnson shows an impressive command of Churchill's writings and speeches from *The World Crisis* and the great and memorable wartime speeches from the summer of 1940 to *Painting as a Pastime*. He tellingly observes that "one of Churchill's strengths, both as a man and a statesman, was that politics never occupied his whole attention and energies," and he appreciates his significant contributions as writer, historian, and as an (amateur) artist of some distinction. But Johnson never analyzes Churchill's writings or speeches at any length. As in *Heroes*, his longest treatment of a literary or historical work is dedicated to a discussion of the mode of composition of Churchill's six-volume war memoirs (*The Second World War*) rather than a discussion of the themes or insights of that work itself (see *Churchill*, 147–51).

of Wilhelmine Germany for succumbing to Nietzsche's false cult of human greatness. German elites, de Gaulle wrote, ignored "the limits marked out by human experience, common sense, and the law." If Johnson had studied de Gaulle's revealing prewar writings—*The Enemy's House Divided* (1924) and *The Edge of the Sword* (1932)—he would have discovered powerful insights into the limits of all ideological projects that ignore the parameters established by "the natural order of things."

Johnson's final chapter focuses on "The Heroic Trinity" who brought down Communism—Ronald Reagan, Margaret Thatcher, and Pope John Paul II—and he has many astute things to say about these three figures. Strangely, however, Johnson presents Reagan as largely bereft of learning and ignorant of some elementary realities of politics—even as he admires the preternatural solidity of his judgments, particularly regarding Communist totalitarianism and the role of government in people's lives. Johnson ignores all of the recently published evidence—Reagan's radio addresses from 1975 to 1979, many of which he wrote himself; his voluminous published correspondence; his White House diaries—that suggest that he was far more than the "booby" of legend. As for Thatcher, whom the author knew well, Johnson emphasizes what is rarely appreciated: that the Iron Lady brought together personal generosity and "tremendous will" in a combination "almost unknown" in public life. Johnson limits himself to four well-crafted pages on John Paul II's role in defeating the Communist behemoth. He concludes that John Paul inhabited "the borderland between the heroic and the saintly," and recognizes that saintliness is a subject for another investigation. But such a man surely belongs in any book on heroism worthy of its name.

The Need for "General Ideas"

Heroes steers clear of larger philosophical reflections on the meaning of human greatness, and perhaps Johnson's Englishness explains why. Tocqueville famously observed that the English have no taste for "general ideas." This is one of the strengths of Britain's moderate and free political order but, alas, one of the weaknesses of its intellectual life. Johnson's book offers no discussion, for instance, of Aristotle's or Cicero's accounts of magnanimity, or a sustained examination of the tensions between goodness and greatness. It skims over or ignores the key writings not just of Churchill and de Gaulle, but also of other democratic statesmen—Lincoln and the American founders come to mind—who thought deeply about greatness and moderation in a democratic age. For a fuller discussion of these themes, one must turn elsewhere. A remarkable recent book by Boston College political theorist Robert Faulkner, *The Case for Greatness: Honorable Ambition and Its Critics*, is a good place to start.

Faulkner's starting point is the "big divide" between "thoughtful citizens" and "appreciative historians" who still acknowledge those great statesmen whose qualities of soul are indispensable for "defending, reforming, and founding a free country," and the various theorists (John Rawls and his students among them) who have succumbed to skepticism, cynicism, and doctrinaire egalitarianism regarding the great and the good. In the tradition of Leo Strauss, Faulkner establishes that the commonsense distinctions between honorable ambition, time-serving mediocrity, and the truly rapacious kind of ambition shorn of "justice, love, nobility, and friendship" are essential to any reasonable comprehension of human affairs. Drawing on Plato's, Xenophon's, and Aristotle's insights into ambition and its limits, Faulkner recovers the fundamental and enduring difference between the ambition of a noble statesman such as Lincoln, who aimed to be worthy of the esteem of his fellow citizens, and the imperial ambition of a Cyrus the Great or Napoleon that gradually became indistinguishable from "cold despotism."

In contrast, Johnson's *Heroes* limits itself to instructing through "example." Johnson is a delight to read because he writes well and understands human nature as it reveals itself in the cauldron of history. His humane voice occasionally goes awry, but he never loses sight of the intimate connection between moral courage, true heroism, and respect for the dignity of man. By providing vivid and concrete illustrations of the ambiguity inherent in human greatness, his work encourages us to admire what is truly admirable while remaining suspicious of that false greatness that scorns justice and genuine nobility.

4

Churchill on Civilization and Its Discontents

Winston Churchill was among the most memorable and inspiring actors in the great and terrible drama that marked the first half of the twentieth century. But as we have seen, he was a man of thought as well as a man of action. Forty-five years after his death, his writings continue to provide unique resources for understanding the threats to civilization in modern times and the essential choiceworthiness of what he did not hesitate to call liberal and Christian civilization.

Almost everyone appreciates the extraordinary role that Churchill's wartime rhetoric played in inspiriting the British nation when it stood alone against the Nazi menace. Moreover, Churchill's fierce and eloquent words were an inspiration to all who valued human liberty and who had the good sense to discern the effectual truth of the "New World Order" proffered by Hitler and his minions. It is entirely appropriate, then, that we continue to pay tribute to the eloquence and heroism of the "last lion," "the largest human being of our time," as Sir Isaiah Berlin so memorably called him.

It is not altogether inaccurate to emphasize the *anachronistic* character of Churchill's model of statesmanship. He brought Plutarchian virtues and an aristocratic sense of human possibilities to bear on the great drama of politics and war in the twentieth century. His keen historical imagination certainly prepared him to play an eminent, and an eminently salutary, role in the "Thirty Years War" which dominated the first half of that century. But it is a mistake to reduce Churchill, as many historians and commentators are prone to do, to the status of a "romantic" whose idiom and temperament no longer speak to the needs and concerns of a democratic age.

To begin with, such an approach presumes that democracy can do without a statesmanship that necessarily takes some of its inspiration from the "greatness" of the past. As importantly, it fails to do justice to Churchill because it doesn't begin to take seriously the thought that informed his partisanship on behalf of civilization. Churchill could be so effective in rousing democratic hearts and minds only because he had a deep appreciation of the vices as well as the virtues that were attendant to the democratic dispensation. As Allan Bloom has noted, Churchill was without doubt an anachronism in the limited sense that his thought and action had roots deep in the soil of the predemocratic Western tradition. But they were also informed by an acute awareness of what can be called the "problem of democracy." Churchill acted nobly on behalf of the liberal democratic regime even as he maintained his critical distance from some of its more problematic tendencies and presuppositions. Let us turn now to the peroration of the "Finest Hour" speech, where Churchill's unforced combination of thoughtfulness and spiritedness is nowhere more in evidence.

THE "FINEST HOUR" SPEECH

The "Finest Hour" speech was delivered on the same day—June 18, 1940—that Charles de Gaulle broadcast his famous radio "Appeal" to the French nation with the full support of Churchill and the British authorities. This remarkable pair of speeches by the two greatest European statesmen of the twentieth century marked the effective end of the "Battle of France" and the beginning of what Churchill was to call the "Battle of Britain." The Battle of Britain was more than a struggle for the survival of an independent British polity. It was, Churchill insisted, nothing less than the essential precondition for the survival of Western civilization and the eventual restoration of European liberty. The ultimate restoration of the freedom and independence of all the captive peoples of Europe depended upon the ability of the British people to withstand the aerial bombardment of the *Luftwaffe* and to ward off the prospect of an imminent land invasion by German military forces.

In the peroration of his June 18 address Churchill not only utilized his formidable rhetorical abilities to draw forth the heroism of a free people but also provided a lucid analysis of what was at stake in the deadly battle between Hitlerism and British democracy. Churchill's words are worthy of extended citation:

What General Weygand has called the Battle of France is over. I expect that the Battle of Britain is about to begin. Upon this battle depends the survival of Christian civilization. Upon it depends our own British life, and the long continuity of our institutions and our Empire. The whole fury and might of the enemy must very soon be turned on us. Hitler knows that he will have to break us in this Island or lose the war. If we can stand up to him, all Europe may be free and the life of the world may move forward into broad, sunlit uplands. But if we fail, then the whole world, including the United States, including all we have known and cared for, will sink into the abyss of a new Dark Age made more sinister, and perhaps more protracted, by the lights of perverted science. Let us therefore brace ourselves to our duties, and so bear ourselves that, if the British Empire and its Commonwealth last for a thousand years, men will say, "This was their finest hour."

There is much that can be said about this extraordinary peroration. More than one commentator has compared it to Henry V's St. Crispin's Day speech in Shakespeare's *Henry V.* The comparison is apt. But while Shakespeare appeals to the pride of a small "band of brothers," Churchill attempts to connect with the inchoate nobility of a free people with little taste for the martial or heroic virtues. He has to rouse their collective will. But what is more striking about Churchill's call to democratic honor is the intellectual analysis upon which it rests. Churchill draws the sharpest contrast between civilization and a new kind of totalitarian despotism. This despotism set out not only to abolish public liberties but also to destroy the wellsprings of civilization. Churchill fully appreciated that Nazi despotism entailed something much more than an atavistic return to the "Dark Ages." It was in the decisive respects a product of intellectual and political modernity. Its lupine imperialism and willful disregard for the inheritance of the European past had little in common with barbarism, traditionally understood. As Churchill put it in his impressive "Arms and the Covenant" speech of December 3, 1936, Nazism, like its *frère-ennemi*, Communism, was a secular religion, "a non-God religion" which "waged wars with the weapons of the twentieth century." The two major totalitarian political religions of the twentieth century rejected the moral inheritance of Western civilization and "substitute[d] the devil for God and hatred for love."

Churchill never succumbed to the illusion of those self-declared "realists" who reassured themselves and others that Hitler was pursuing the "national interest" of Germany—if in a somewhat overwrought and distasteful manner.* Churchill

---

* But this lifelong anti-Communist, who immediately understood the threat

avoided this error precisely because he appreciated the terrible originality of modern totalitarianism and its ambition to engineer human souls by utilizing the full resources of a science subordinated to ideological ends. Moreover, his evocation of an imperiled "civilization" was more than a rhetorical flourish. In his great wartime speeches, Churchill freely appealed to both liberal democracy and Christian ethics as the indispensable moral bases of resistance to Nazi tyranny. His emphasis was always on the "continuity" of a Western civilization that acknowledged the sacred demands of mercy and justice as well as the inviolable rights and dignity of free human beings. In the West's mortal struggle with totalitarianism, it was necessary to affirm *both* the traditional resources of Western freedom and its claim to be the authentic embodiment of modern liberty. It was for this reason that Churchill regularly exhorted his compatriots to defend both liberal and Christian civilization against what Herman Rauschning had famously called "the revolution of nihilism." It was the survival of that dual civilized patrimony that was the ultimate stake in the conflict between an ascendant Germany and the remnant of the liberal European order.

An examination of Churchill's political speeches in the period immediately preceding World War II (during his so-called Wilderness Years of political exile in the 1930s) reveals the underlying coherence of his intellectual reflections on politics, civilization, and modern totalitarianism. A somewhat cursory raid into those speeches will allow us to more fully identify the intellectual underpinnings of Churchill's wartime political rhetoric.

---

that Lenin's Bolshevik regime posed to the civilized world, falsely assumed during the Second World War that Stalin was merely a Russian tsar in ideological disguise. In the course of the common struggle against Nazi Germany, Churchill wanted to believe that Stalin stood, however perversely, for the ambitions and interests of a great people. He thus succumbed for a time to the temptation of conflating things Russian and Soviet.

CIVILIZATION AND ITS DISCONTENTS

Churchill's most complete and satisfying reflection on the meaning of *civilization* can be found in an address of that name that he delivered at the University of Bristol on July 2, 1938.[1] In that speech he defined civilization as the aspiration toward a lawful and peaceful society, marked by the subordination of warriors and despots to civilian authority. Churchill's Whig "progressivism," if one calls it that, also incorporated an understanding of civilized liberty as a tradition or inheritance that must be safeguarded anew by each generation. He fused a liberal commitment to progress with a conservative recognition of the moral and political indispensability of civilizing tradition. He defined the principles of civilization that culminate in a *tradition* of constitutionalism. Churchill writes:

> What does [Civilization] mean? It means a society based upon the opinion of civilians. It means that violence, the rule of warriors and despotic chiefs, the condition of camps and warfare, of riot and tyranny, give place to parliaments where laws are made, and independent courts of justice in which over long periods those laws are maintained. That is Civilization—and in its soil grow continually freedom, comfort, and culture. When Civilization reigns in any country, a wider and less harassed life is afforded to the masses of the people. The traditions of the people are cherished, and the inheritance bequeathed to us by former wise and valiant men becomes a rich estate to be enjoyed by all.
>
> The central principle of Civilization is the subordination of the ruling authority to the settled customs of the people and to their will as expressed through the Constitution.

74

Civilization is not a once-and-for-all achievement, an unearned dispensation of fate, or a product of the march of historical necessity. It is, rather, an inheritance that is always threatened by the atavistic temptations of barbarism and today by "the lights of perverted science," to cite the memorable formulation from Churchill's "Finest Hour" speech.

The idealistic illusion is to confuse the millennial-long development of a civilized way of life with the thoroughgoing pacification of the international order; the mistake of the realist, in contrast, is to assume that "the same principles which have shaped the free, ordered, tolerant civilization of the British Isles and British empire" could not be "found serviceable in the organization" of the larger world. Churchill envisions an international order where the rule of law would gradually become the foundation of international as well as national life. But this is a "supreme hope" that scarcely begins to describe the realities of a conflict-ridden and anxious world. This hope can begin to become a reality only when (as Churchill put it in "Arms and the Covenant") the free peoples of the world "rally and invite under the League of Nations the greatest number of strongly armed nations" that can be marshaled for that task. To be sure, Churchill had no illusions about the League of Nations. Its failure to deter aggression and its questionable fidelity to its own principles were apparent to all with eyes to see. But he was convinced that international law, supported by the full military might of peace-loving nations, could provide moral legitimacy for collective security in a world imperiled by new forms of totalitarian aggression.

It was not that Churchill rejected the traditional idea of the "balance of power." Instead, he wished to build upon this pillar of British statecraft while transforming it in the process. In a well-known address delivered in March 1936 to the Conservative Backbench Foreign Affairs Committee of the House of Commons, Churchill lauded Britain's four-hundred-year policy of standing up to "the continental military tyrant whoever he was, whatever nation he led." It was this commitment to the European balance of power and to the liberties of the smaller nations of Europe that prevented Philip II, Louis XIV, and Napoleon in turn from each becoming the master of Europe. Churchill freely appealed to this "wonderful unconscious tradition of British foreign policy" in an effort to stir his own party from its quiescence before a resurgent and militarized German Reich. Many of Churchill's Conservative colleagues were wary of adopting an excessively critical stance toward Germany while others clearly detested Bolshevism more than they loathed Hitler. Churchill's task was to remind the governing Conservatives of their responsibilities as the custodians of a tradition of foreign policy that had never hesitated to confront "the strongest, most aggressive, most dominant Power" on the European continent. No "military, political, economic, or scientific fact" had altered "the justice, wisdom, valour, and Prudence upon which our ancestors acted." And nothing "has happened to human nature" to make power political considerations obsolete. That was the enduring insight of the realist tradition of European statecraft, an insight that was being ignored in a misguided effort to appease a revolutionary state with limitless ambitions.

In the March 1936 speech, Churchill observed that Britain's traditional policy took no account of which nation "seeks the overlordship of Europe." This unarticulated tradition could afford to abstract from the clash of regimes and ideologies: it was "concerned solely with whoever is the strongest or potentially dominating tyrant." Such eminent authorities as Hans J. Morgenthau and Henry Kissinger have thus concluded that Churchill, too, must have abstracted from any serious consideration of the internal characteristics of regimes when analyzing the motives and behavior of state actors. Their Churchill is a "realist" *avant la lettre* who knew that the calculation of the balance of power was the alpha and the omega of international relations. But neither Morgenthau nor Kissinger read Churchill's speech with sufficient sensitivity to its political context. Moreover, they detached his opening discussion of traditional British policy from the argument of the speech as a whole. Even in his speech to the Conservative backbenchers, Churchill went out of his way to highlight the "peace-loving," "parliamentary," and "liberal" character of the British and French democracies as well as the totalitarian character of Hitler's regime. In contrast to Britain's traditional policy, Churchill was necessarily preoccupied with the struggle of regimes and ideologies. He implicitly recognized the distinction between an international order where all the actors accepted the rules of the game and deferred to common principles of civilized order, and one where the destiny of humankind was the very stake of foreign policy. In marked contrast to the conservative-minded democracies, Germany posed a threat to the integrity of the international order. She was now dominated by a "handful of desperadoes" who respected neither the liberties of their own people nor the elementary prerequisites of international law.

In the course of his speech, Churchill therefore quietly transformed and "moralized" the balance of power tradition by making it the historical antecedent of the noble idea that he called "the Covenant and Arms." He emphasized that "the fostering and fortifying of the League of Nations" was the best way to defend Britain's island security and was perfectly in accord with her democratic principles and commitment to settling disputes by "patient discussion." In addition, Churchill warned against a cynical underestimation of "the force which these ideals exert upon British democracy." He thus signaled that power politics operates in a new historical context and should not disregard the moral aspirations of democratic peoples toward a more lawful international order. But law and morality are, of course, insufficient. The British and French democracies must provide the political leadership and military might to make the covenant of the League of Nations more than a sweet-sounding declaration or a cover for utopian delusions about a world without conflict or war. The two great democracies of Western Europe are the indispensable core of the new international framework. They must be willing to exercise their power on behalf of freedom and justice even if that framework were to break down completely.

All in all, Churchill fully appreciated that parliamentary democracies have "tremendous inhibitions against aggressive war" but at the same time they must be willing to arm to maintain the peace. He recommended that a full array of older and newer instruments of statecraft be put at the service of preserving civilization against the ideological tyrannies committed to its destruction. Churchill's capacious moral realism has a place for the balance of power *and* collective security, for a powerful Royal Navy *and* a vigorous conception of international law.

In his March 1936 address, Churchill discreetly took aim at false realists who ignore the inescapable place of moral principle in the conduct of democratic foreign policy. In the 1938 "Civilization" address, he criticized misguided idealists who take the fragile achievement of civilization for granted. The antepenultimate and penultimate paragraphs of his short address delineate the essential preconditions of an idealism worthy of its name:

> But it is vain to imagine that that the mere perception or declaration of right principles, whether in one country or many countries, will be of any value unless they are supported by those qualities of civic virtue and manly courage—aye, and by those instruments and agencies of force and science which in the last resort must be the defense of right and reason.
>
> Civilization will not last, freedom will not survive, peace will not be kept, unless a very large majority of mankind unite

together to defend them and show themselves possessed of a constabulary force before which barbaric and atavistic forces will stand in awe.

These powerful remarks will especially resonate with readers of *The Gathering Storm* (1948). In that work, the first volume of *The Second World War*, Churchill excoriated the "pathetic belief" that love could ever be the foundation of peace. In his riveting narrative, he chronicled the failure of the British political class to provide the requisite moral and political leadership in the years after 1933. Confronted with a dictatorship that rejected Christian ethics and made a mockery of international law, the democracies prevaricated before one provocation after another and allowed Germany to systematically rearm and then to establish its political and military dominance over the European continent. Churchill famously characterized the "theme" of that volume as follows: "HOW THE ENGLISH-SPEAKING PEOPLES THROUGH THEIR UNWISDOM, CARELESSNESS, AND GOOD NATURE ALLOWED THE WICKED TO REARM."

His dramatic account of how the "unnecessary war" came to pass was as much an indictment of the easygoing acquiescence of democratic peoples in the rise of German power as it was a critique of the ruthlessness of Hitler and the Nazis. What makes *The Gathering Storm* of particular interest to students of politics and political philosophy is Churchill's penetrating analysis of how "the structure and habits of democratic States" seemingly "lack those elements of persistence and conviction that can give security to humble masses." Churchill suggests that "public opinion" is the reigning god of the democratic order and that it rarely defers to uncomfortable truths even when national self-preservation is at stake. Moreover, a commercial people is more likely to respond to the siren calls of humanitarianism than to the stern demands of manly courage. In order to rouse his contemporaries from their lethargy, Churchill recalled ancient precedents and drew attention to those aspects of the Western experience that were necessarily less present to democratic peoples. This appeal to "the wisdom of the past" is nowhere more apparent than in his parliamentary address of October 5, 1938. In that speech Churchill challenged the euphoria that accompanied Chamberlain's return from Munich and called the Anglo-French capitulation by its name: "A total and unmitigated defeat."

"Tak[ing] Our Stand for Freedom as in the Olden Time"

The Munich Pact speech is in many respects the Churchillian speech par excellence. Churchill places his critique of the capitulation of the democracies at Munich in the larger context of a searing indictment of appeasement and all its works. He shows that the abandonment of Czechoslovakia, the only remaining democratic state in East-Central Europe (and a faithful adherent to the League of Nations at that), was the logical consequence of a foreign policy that had woefully neglected national defenses and had pursued "the line of least resistance" when confronted by clear evidence of Germany's malign intentions. Churchill's damning indictment of British policy was a lightning bolt that pierced through the climate of self-congratulation that was enveloping the Parliament, the press, and the nation as a whole. In retrospect, it provided him with valuable moral capital that would do much to bolster his authority during the critical opening years of the Second World War. In his Munich Pact speech, Churchill illustrated "the firmness of character . . . unmoved by currents of opinion" that he himself considered the hallmark of true statesmanship. He refused "to court political popularity" precisely because he wished to provide necessary if unwelcome counsel to a nation that had come to confuse capitulation to evil with the honest and patient search for peaceful solutions to international problems.

In the first part of his speech, Churchill exposed the fatuousness of the claim that the abandonment of their Czechoslovakian ally was the price that the democracies had to pay for "the saving of peace" in Europe. He readily acknowledged that there is never any absolute guarantee against the outbreak of war. But both prudence and justice demanded that the democracies maintain faith with the Czechoslovakian people by offering them a guarantee of support in the case of a German invasion. This "third alternative" between immediate war and capitulation to Hitler's demands may well have stirred anti-Nazi elements in the German military to action (we know from *The Gathering Storm* that Churchill was aware at the time of the efforts of General Franz Halder in that regard) and would have guaranteed that thirty badly needed Czechoslovakian divisions would be available for combat in the event of the outbreak of a general European war. Instead, Britain and France offered a (worthless) security guarantee to a dispirited and dismembered Czech state only after it had been thoroughly undermined by the territorial concessions imposed upon it at Munich. In his remarks to Parliament, Churchill predicted the imminent demise of an independent Czechoslovakian state with uncanny accuracy. (The march of German troops into Prague on March 15, 1939, would trigger an Anglo-French guarantee to a Poland that was significantly less able to defend itself than Czechoslovakia had been.) Churchill convincingly argued that the pusillanimity of the democracies only served to bring Europe closer to war and to leave Britain and France even more vulnerable when the moment of truth arrived.

Moreover, the democracies had shamelessly allowed Hitler to manipulate the democratic "principle of self-determination" in order to justify the incorporation of several million Sudeten Germans within a totalitarian state without their express consent. Churchill directed his ire at the moral corruption that accompanied this policy of peace at any price. Instead of "standing firm upon the front of law" and defending "the orderly remedy of grievances," the democracies were led to accept essentially totalitarian conceptions of peace and self-determination. Such were the consequences of good intentions severed from a manly willingness to fight for freedom. Such were the consequences of the "realist" identification of Nazi imperialism with the remedying of legitimate German grievances.

As the central part of his speech makes clear, Churchill feared that the acceptance of the Nazi domination of Europe would create an atmosphere radically inhospitable to the survival of Britain's principles and ways of life. Dominating the continent as a whole, Nazi Germany certainly would enter a new, more radical, and totalitarian phase of political existence. The war against conservatives, liberals, democrats, patriots, Christians, and especially Jews would surely intensify. The pressure for England to accommodate herself to the National Socialists' "new world order" might in time become overwhelming. At a minimum, "responsible" people would avoid saying or doing anything that might offend the German authorities. Self-censorship would become the order of the day.

Churchill, of course, adamantly rejected any hint of moral capitulation to National Socialism. He continued to insist that there could "never be friendship between the British democracy and the Nazi power, that power which spurns Christian ethics, which cheers its onward course by a barbarous paganism, which derives strength and perverted pleasure from persecution, and uses, as we have seen, with pitiless barbarity the threat of murderous force."

The appeasers' prudence, marked by the desire to avoid war at all costs, could lead only to what Churchill elsewhere calls the "bull's eye of disaster." Such blind acquiescence to evil would not only fail to prevent war but would ultimately destroy the moral integrity of the British people.

Churchill advocated another road for Britain. He saw hope in "the supreme recovery of moral health and martial vigor" by Britons' taking their "stand for freedom as in the olden time," to cite the stirring peroration of his speech. In rhetoric that effortlessly melded the language of the biblical prophet and the classical statesman, Churchill told his listeners that they have experienced only the "first foretaste of a bitter cup which will be proffered" to them unless they fortify themselves at the spirited wells of their patrimony. The preservation of civilization depends upon those "qualities of civic virtue and manly courage" that are, always and everywhere, indispensable supports of human freedom. Earlier in his speech, Churchill cited the authority of the tenth-century *Anglo-Saxon Chronicle* in this regard and reminded his listeners that "all wisdom is not new wisdom." There were lessons to be learned even today from studying the sorry reign of King Ethelred the Unready, who squandered the "strong position" he inherited "from the descendants of King Alfred" and left England prostrate before the invading Danes.

Conclusion

Churchill's thought and rhetoric freely drew upon elements of ancient and modern theory and practice, power politics and the rule of law, and liberal and Christian civilization in a comprehensive effort to awaken democratic peoples from their somnolence. This man of peace was willing to prepare for war in order to safeguard the inheritance of civilization itself. Churchill's statesmanship was informed by a deep appreciation of the achievement and fragility of civilization and of the dependence of modern democracy on traditional moral and civic resources that his contemporaries were all too hesitant to acknowledge. As we have seen, Churchill's thoughtful appreciation of the "problem of democracy" is particularly evident in his 1925 essay "Mass Effects in Modern Life," an essay that can be found in his delightful 1932 collection *Thoughts and Adventures*. Through his thought and deed, this humane antitotalitarian statesman encouraged citizens of modern democracies to draw precious civic and spiritual resources from a tradition of civilization that is broader and deeper than the modern ideology of "the rights of man."

Part III

The False Allure of "Pure Democracy"

5

1968 and the Meaning of Democracy

The year 1968 witnessed not only unprecedented unrest in the streets and on college campuses but also a truly global challenge to liberal civilization in the form of what was then widely called the New Left. Denouncing bourgeois capitalism and bureaucratic state socialism alike, the theoreticians and activists of the New Left dreamed of a new civilization without repressive hierarchies or restraints. The spirit of '68 was essentially antinomian and gave rise to a "culture of repudiation" (as Roger Scruton has called it) that has decisively transformed academic and intellectual life throughout the Western world over the course of the last forty years. Although 1968 did not succeed as a political project, at least not immediately (it came closest to succeeding in France), it did inaugurate, or powerfully reinforce, a bold cultural project to subvert or "deconstruct" authoritative cultural, political, and religious traditions in the name of liberation and autonomy, the guiding values of the new cultural dispensation. As importantly, it marked that moment when Europeans in particular ceased to define themselves as caretakers of "liberal and Christian civilization," to evoke the wartime rhetoric of essentially conservative, antitotalitarian statesmen such as Winston Churchill and Charles de Gaulle. The postmodern West increasingly defines liberty in terms of the single imperative of consent.

It brashly dismisses, when not ignoring, the classical and Christian features of Western liberty. If I am correct, 1968 is of much more than symbolic importance. It is that crucial turning point when modern democracy lost consciousness of civilized liberty as a precious *inheritance* to be preserved.

If '68 was a global phenomenon par excellence, it reached a revealing fever pitch in France in the "May events" that shook that country to the core. During a visit to France in May 2008, I had an opportunity to witness the ongoing French commemorations of the May events, filled as they were with nostalgia and the lost promise of revolutionary youth. Parisian bookstores· prominently displayed a massive literature on those events, while magazines were filled with uncritical evocations of the three or four weeks that are said to have changed the world. *Le Monde*, the house journal of the establishment Left, went so far as to reproduce, each day, the front page of the newspaper on the parallel day in May 1968. Those old front pages perfectly captured both the obligatory leftism and the indulgence toward "Youth" that dominated that venerable paper's response to the implosion of the French social and political order. One article by Maurice Duverger was representative of the atmosphere of 1968: that once famous political scientist cheerfully seconded the student movement's call for the abolition of exams, since examinations took professors away from precious scientific research and at the same time reinforced the alienation of the young. In the giddy, carnival-like atmosphere of the time, this passed for serious analysis.

Today, a majority of the French (or at least of the French intellectual class)—and not all of them on the Left—look back nostalgically to the turning point that was May 1968. Some of this is the self-indulgence of a generation that is no longer so young. Some of it is compensation by a Left that now reluctantly admits that revolution, even of a mimetic kind, is no longer a serious option for France and Europe. But the commemorative character of the French response to the fortieth anniversary of the May events risks obscuring the farcical dimensions of that eruption; more seriously, it risks obscuring 1968's truly revolutionary and ideological dimensions as well. Lost in the celebration of 1968 as the birth pangs of an unproblematic "postmodern democracy" is a concrete feel for the nature of the event itself.

A GLOBAL PHENOMENON

We often forget that 1968 was a truly global phenomenon. Americans easily recall Berkeley and Columbia, and Europeans recall Paris and the Sorbonne. But that momentous year also saw unrest in Dakar, Mexico City, Tokyo, and elsewhere; the rise of a revolutionary New Left throughout the Western world; and, in a different key, the quasi-miraculous "Prague Spring" in Soviet-dominated Czechoslovakia. The Prague Spring gave undue hope to some on the Left that Leninist-Stalinist tyranny could be transformed into "socialism with a human face."

There were both general and particular causes at work. The events of 1968 surely had deep roots in cultural and social developments that were in the process of transforming the entire Western world. After the Second Vatican Council (1962–1965), for example, the Roman Catholic Church suffered from self-inflicted wounds. That hoary institution transformed itself seemingly overnight from an authoritative bastion of traditional wisdom to a church in apparent freefall. Its progressive elements did not hesitate "to kneel before the world," celebrating socialism and revolution, secular humanitarianism, and every allegedly democratic development in society at large. In America, the moral promise of the civil-rights movement, rooted in an appeal to American principles of liberty and equality bolstered by biblical religion, was coopted by the Black Power movement and other manifestations of identity politics. The Women's Liberation movement and the recently manufactured birth-control pill (it was introduced in France in 1967) conspired, for better or worse, to sever sexuality from a natural order and individual liberty from its larger familial and social contexts. In France, social institutions as diverse as the Church and the Boy Scouts scrambled to adopt less hierarchical "power structures" in the years immediately before 1968. Everywhere an ideology of liberation challenged the old bourgeois ethos of self-command and self-control. The explosion of 1968 was in some important respects a dramatic process already well under way rather than the unanticipated announcement of a new world.

MAY 1968

Despite these major social and cultural transformations, nothing in France seemed particularly out of the ordinary on the eve of May 1968. No one anticipated that ongoing disputes about the organization of the French university system would give rise to momentous social and political upheavals. Unrest at the University of Nanterre, fueled by the activism of anarchist revolutionaries led by Daniel Cohn-Bendit, soon spread to the Sorbonne. In the days after May 3, that august institution was more or less commandeered by student radicals. Students clashed with police even as they—and sympathetic professors—"contested" the traditional structures of state and society. Student protesters combined violence with a festive atmosphere celebrating their emancipation from traditional educational obligations and social and cultural restraints. In the face of this rapidly deteriorating situation (and of public opinion's remarkable indulgence toward the student revolutionaries), the government of Prime Minister Georges Pompidou began to lose nerve.

The initial student phase of the May events was followed by a nationwide general strike of up to ten million workers that lasted two weeks and shut down the economic life of the country. This economic phase of the crisis was followed by a political phase that lasted from May 27 until May 30. For the first time, it looked like the strong, self-respecting constitutional order inaugurated by Charles de Gaulle in 1958 might collapse under the combined assaults of a student revolution, a general strike, and the machinations of leftist political forces. A takeover by the Communist Party and other Popular Front forces became a real possibility for the first time. It was only on May 30 that France began to step back from the abyss.

After initial hesitations—and a lackluster television address on May 24—President de Gaulle seized the initiative with a truly decisive radio address to the nation on May 30, 1968.[1] He announced his decision to dissolve the National Assembly and to call for elections. He denounced the "intimidation, intoxication, and tyranny" exercised by various revolutionary groups as well as the danger posed by a "party which is a totalitarian enterprise." He lamented the fact that as a result of this intimidation teachers were prevented from teaching, students from studying, and workers from working. And he reassured the French people that "the Republic will not abdicate." Hundreds of thousands of citizens responded to de Gaulle's radio address by descending on the Champs Élysées for a massive rally in support of the Republic. The tide had now turned. The general strike began to run out of steam.

It took another couple of weeks (and three "nights of the barricades") for order to be restored to the Sorbonne and the Left Bank. In the elections at the end of June, the Gaullists for the first time won an absolute majority in the National Assembly. Things had come full circle.

We have noted that revolutionaries of the Left (Trotskyites and Maoists of various stripes) played a major role in radicalizing the student movement. These subterranean revolutionary "groupuscules" outmaneuvered the Communist Party and claimed to speak for the young as a whole. Some of these militants (André Glucksmann, Bernard-Henri Lévy, and the other "new philosophers" of media fame come to mind) later broke with revolutionary ideology and became vocal defenders of "the rights of man." These *soixante-huitards* ('68ers) now tend to read their own intellectual and political trajectory into the nature of the event itself. They remain partisans of 1968 even in their new centrist or even conservative incarnations. But in truth there is an element of bad faith and wishful thinking informing the libertarian reading of 1968. The supposed libertarianism of 1968 directed nearly all its antiauthoritarian ire at bourgeois society and was remarkably indulgent toward the totalitarianism of the Left. The Marxist consensus so abundantly on display that year did not at the time reflect the slightest clarity about the real nature of Communist totalitarianism. That was to come later, under the impact of Solzhenitsyn's *The Gulag Archipelago*, a work that had a much more dramatic impact in France than anywhere else in the Western world.

ARON'S WITNESS

In retrospect, it is easy to forget the massive abdication of good sense by so many who ought to have known better during the course of the May events. The great exception was the French political philosopher, sociologist, and journalist Raymond Aron. His columns in *Le Figaro* and his lively, eloquent, and insightful book *La révolution introuvable* (*The Elusive Revolution*) were beacons of clarity and civic courage in the midst of the "revolutionary psychodrama" (as he pointedly called it at the time). Aron was the first to expose the "imitative" character of students and intellectuals play-acting at revolution, risking the destruction of bourgeois society and the liberal university with little or nothing constructive to offer in their place. He recalled Flaubert's and Tocqueville's powerful critiques of the revolution of 1848 (where a similar "literary politics" guided the pseudo-Jacobins of that time) to highlight the French propensity to make revolution in the place of a serious effort to bring about reforms. A man of remarkably balanced judgment, Aron was angered by the inability and unwillingness of those in positions of responsibility to resist the delirium of the time. In *The Elusive Revolution* he eloquently defends his refusal to "take too seriously" the various actors in the "revolutionary comedy":

> I refuse to salute our "admirable youth." Too many grown men have done so. Barricades which are symbolically effective seem to me to be neither an intellectual nor a moral achievement. If young people have some exalted memory of the barricades, well and good. Why should old people be obliged to counterfeit sentiments which they do not feel? If the young denounce the brutality of the C.R.S. (the French riot police) while in the same breath preaching the cult of violence themselves, the contradiction seems to me to be nothing more than a good technique of subversion. But men of my generation or of the generation after do not want to feel that they were caught up in what I persist in calling collective madness. They do not accept that they are out of their minds.

Aron had long been a critic of the overcentralized and overcrowded French university system and had even left his teaching position at the Sorbonne "in disgust," as he put it, some months before May '68. And while he respected General de Gaulle as an authentically great man, he freely acknowledged the limits of Gaullist hauteur, the quasi-monarchical style that had set the

93

tone for the French Fifth Republic. He was also critical of the civil-service authoritarianism of the Fifth Republic's governing class and of the quasi-neutralist bent of French foreign policy.

In Aron's view, the Fifth Republic was nonetheless a *liberal* order that respected fundamental political and personal liberties. But its approach to governing was excessively aloof and oligarchic and thus insufficiently "republican" in character. A necessary strengthening of executive authority—woefully absent under the French Third and Fourth Republics—had led to an excessive depoliticization of French society. Still, if Aron could not simply accept the Gaullist vision of France he personally felt "closer to the Gaullists than to their opponents." He was "deeply wounded by" 1968's "radical negation of patriotism and by the substitution of the name of Che Guevara for that of a resistance hero [Charles de Gaulle]."

Unfortunately, Aron's voice was largely absent from the French commemoration of the May events (although the distinguished French quarterly *Commentaire*, founded by Aron in 1978, published an excerpt from *La révolution introuvable* and two broadly Aronian reflections on the May events in its Summer 2008 issue). This relative absence of Aron's perspective in the contemporary debate is problematic for several reasons. Aron's writings on 1968 serve as a powerful corrective to the French tendency to become "obsessed by their memories or the myths of their past" and to mistake "riots and disorder" in the streets of Paris "for a Promethean exploit," in Aron's words. In addition, Aron's writings on 1968 make abundantly clear what was at stake in the final revolutionary days of May before de Gaulle's May 30 radio address awoke the good sense of France's silent majority.

There were only two plausible *political* alternatives to the Fifth Republic. The first was the rule of a "totalitarian enterprise," the Communist Party, which had been driven by the power vacuum at the end of May to call for a "popular government" (a government of the Left, dominated by the Communist Party). The second possibility was the establishment of a Sixth French Republic headed by an official of the non-Communist Left such as François Mitterrand or Pierre Mendès-France. Such a republic would be the product of lawlessness and would be "truly unworthy" of a self-respecting people and nation. As we have seen, Aron was ambivalent about the established political regime in France. Yet he vigorously supported the continuity of the legal government. The Gaullist republic "was based on universal suffrage" and did not violate "fundamental liberties." All of the available political alternatives—generalized lawlessness, Communist despotism, or a power play by the opposition—were much less acceptable.

One can continue this sort of analysis. The distinguished French historian Alain Besançon has written a masterly memoir on May '68 that appeared in the Summer 2008 issue of *Commentaire*. As Besançon observes, the Communist Party did not really want revolution. In part it feared the abyss opened up by a truly revolutionary situation; in part the French Communist Party and its Soviet masters were broadly satisfied with de Gaulle's independent foreign policy. There was an implicit pact between the Gaullists and the Communists that had served to maintain order in France. But at the time there was no guarantee that that pact would hold. And, in fact, after May 27, the pact had dangerously frayed. The Communists, stung by the opposition of their own rank-and-file union members to the Grenelle accords (dramatic concessions offered by the Pompidou government to put an end to the general strike) and by revolutionary agitation on the ultra-Left, were increasingly prepared to cross the Rubicon—to engage in real revolutionary action. De Gaulle was not being demagogic in his speech to the nation on May 30: he genuinely feared that a Communist takeover was a distinct possibility in France. On the eve of the May 30 address, such anti-Communist stalwarts (and critics of May '68) as Aron, Annie Kriegel, and Alain Besançon seriously contemplated the possibility of going into exile if everything was indeed lost. Elegiac French accounts of 1968 as a legitimate democratic protest against Gaullist authoritarianism and the stifling conformities of a hierarchical social order therefore grossly obscure the political stakes of the May events. Nineteen sixty-eight was much more than an "eruption of the social"—of democratic "softness" and the power of civil society—as so many analysts suggest today. In May 1968 a "revolutionary psychodrama"—a seemingly harmless talkfest—brought France, and France alone in the Western world, perilously close to a genuine revolutionary conflagration.

The Thought of '68

Besançon has perceptively noted the yawning gap between the heady language in which the actors of 1968 expressed themselves and the "uniformity" of that event's consequences. Understanding that gap is crucial to deciphering the "mystery" and "ambiguity" of 1968. The May events did not have a single or uniform profile. The remarkably juvenile slogans—"Demand the impossible," "It is forbidden to forbid," "Take your desires for realities"—in themselves are without any serious intellectual interest or content. They are, however, revealing popular expressions of a deep-seated antinomianism connected to the thought underlying 1968.

To the extent that the movement had a coherent ideological profile, it can be found in the conjunction of the philosophy current in France in the 1960s—structuralist, Byzantine, obscure—with a diffuse leftist ideology that paid homage to Mao, Trotsky, and Castro. This ideology had its hard core in the revolutionary "groupuscules" mentioned above, who played a major role in radicalizing events in both the universities and the factories.

This ideology's soft core was antiauthoritarian and antihierarchical, what might broadly be called "left-libertarian" in orientation. In both its soft and hard manifestations, the radicalism of 1968 evoked a revolutionary alternative to bourgeois society that somehow would not culminate in Soviet-style bureaucratic despotism (by now, the Soviet Union seemed hopelessly petrified or sclerotic to them).

The partisans of 1968 were mesmerized by the vision of direct democracy in an industrial society and appealed to "participation" ("autogestion") as the only legitimate governing principle within every educational, social, economic, and political institution. Authority as such was identified with domination and repression. Of course, this overlooked elementary social realities and necessities. Aron nicely highlights the "scorn for facts," for elementary social realities, that underlay the radically egalitarian vision of the Parisian intellectuals:

> Many higher intellectuals have an incredible scorn for facts. The formula "there are no facts" is much acclaimed in Parisian circles. Of course, I am aware that in a sense this formula is philosophically true. There are no facts which have not been construed from documents by an historian. I am aware of this kind of consideration—after all, I began my career as a philosopher by making speculations of this kind. But when all is said and done at times I am tempted to . . . state that every society is subject to the constraints of fact—the need for production, for organization, for technical hierarchy, the need for techno-bureaucracy and so on. French intellectuals are so subtle that they end up by forgetting the obvious.

In a famous book that has given rise to endless polemics, *La pensée de 68*, the French philosophers Luc Ferry and Alain Renault analyzed "the thought of '68," the antihumanist philosophical currents that preceded, informed, and were given new life by the revolutionary spectacle of that year. Some of Ferry and Renault's critics have vociferously denied that thinkers such as Foucault, Derrida, and Lacan had much of a causal role in the May events. Their writings were too abstract to influence a broader public and some of them (Foucault in particular) were initially skeptical of the students and their motives. But all of this is beside the point. Ferry and Renault did not claim that anti-humanism or sophisticated Parisian nihilism *caused* the May events. They made the more limited and plausible claim that the French philosophy of the 1960s created an atmosphere that nour-ished the spirit of '68 and informed the actions of many of its key players. In important respects, Ferry and Renault were merely developing an insight that Aron had already highlighted in *The Elusive Revolution* (they cite him generously at a crucial moment in their book).

As Aron noted in the midst of the events, Parisian intellec-tuals (with a few notable exceptions) succumbed to nihilism of a particularly crude variety when they confused their "criti-cal function" with an "absolute condemnation of society." They practiced—even perfected—the "literary politics" of the revo-lution of 1848 that had been condemned by Tocqueville in his *Recollections.* Too many preached or tolerated "the cult of pure violence" with no thought of an alternative society except a vague vision of a radiant future without hierarchy or vertical structures of authority. At the same time, the same figures showed limitless indulgence (and fascination) toward murderous tyrants in far-off lands—Mao and Castro among them—about whom they knew little or nothing.

Forsaking the Stalinism of old, Parisian intellectuals suc-cumbed to a *gauchisme* tinged by the fashionable intellectual nihilism of the day. And in the midst of the crisis, the "cult of action" associated with the existentialist-cum-Marxist Jean-Paul

Sartre made a (temporary) comeback on the streets of Paris. Aron writes:

> The god of the intellectuals of the sixties was no longer the Sartre who had dominated the post-war period, but a mixture of Lévi-Strauss, Foucault, Althusser and Lacan. All passed for structuralists, although they were structuralists in different ways. The most refined of the intelligentsia watched Godard's films, read Lacan without understanding him, and swore by the scientificity of Althusser and acclaimed Lévi-Strauss's structuralism. Oddly, some of these avant-garde intellectuals claimed to be scientific with respect to ethnology or economics, but Maoist when it came to action. During the May period the scientificity disappeared and the cult of action, the cult of the cultural revolution, spread in various forms. Sartre and *Dialectical Reason*, the *groupe en fusion*, the revolutionary mob, had taken their revenge on the structure of society.

The intellectuals discussed by Aron showed little regard for the fragility of civilized order. They celebrated every assault on established authority as a victory for personal freedom and authenticity.

One of the defining traits of the New Left everywhere was its conflation of liberty with liberation and its willful refusal to distinguish authority from authoritarianism. Nor was this a passing phase. In the years after the May events, as Roger Kimball and Roger Scruton among others have documented, "the thought of '68" became the official philosophy of the humanities in universities throughout the Western world. The scientism of the structuralists gave way to radical social constructivism and intemperate efforts to subvert—to "deconstruct"—traditional wisdom and established social institutions. Egalitarian moralism coexisted with a fanatical repudiation of the idea of Truth, with a dogmatic insistence that morality and justice have no other supports than the linguistic categories and cultural assumptions of a contingent social order. The academic partisans of deconstruction give no more thought than their forebears in France to the effects of such easygoing nihilism on the capacity of free men and women to live together in a spirit of responsibility and mutual respect. Without some sort of grounding, *equality* and *justice* become will-o'-the-wisps, ideological slogans to express contempt for a reality that does not live up to the languid dreams of demi-intellectuals.

THE "SOCIAL" CONSEQUENCES OF 1968

If the quasi-revolutionaries of '68 failed to replace the existing political order in France, they were far more successful on the social plane. It is a mistake to deny altogether the real benefits that accompanied this upheaval. The democratization of mores; the weakening of heavy-handed "paternalist" authority in the family, Church, and political order; the growing demands for genuine consultation between employers and employees and rulers and the ruled: all these did serve to revitalize the democratic energies of modern society. These developments, legitimate within limits as a corrective to the rigidities of a traditional social order, were, however, well underway before 1968. With the explosions of May they took on a strikingly destructive cast. As the French philosopher and cultural critic Chantal Delsol has pointed out, along with the (qualified) benefits that flowed from the May events came excesses of every kind. New ideologies were committed "to effac[ing] from the earth all the authority of the old societies, with the goal of installing their own." This new authoritarianism was more illiberal than anything found in the old order since it showed limitless contempt for the habits, practices, and judgments that had long served to support civilized human existence.[2]

Alain Besançon also locates the deepest meaning of 1968 in a broadly Tocquevillian framework. Besançon acknowledges that the May movement had elements of psychodrama. Some of its features were indeed "accidental and insignificant." But its deepest meaning only became apparent later. If the American and French revolutions installed democracy in the political realm, "'68 has extended the field of democracy to the whole of the social order." With a comment (and pathos) worthy of Tocqueville, Besançon notes that "the revolution is not finished." By this he means that the "democratic revolution" continues to transform and to undermine every authoritative institution. Everything, including truth itself, must bow before the tribunal of autonomy and consent. Nineteen sixty-eight was that moment when democracy became self-consciously humanitarian and postpolitical and therefore broke with the continuity of Western civilization.

The most convincing interpretations of May '68 bring together Aron's political perspective with a broadly Tocquevillian appreciation for the ongoing effects of the modern democratic revolution. At the time of the May eruption Aron hesitated to endorse André Malraux's interpretation of it as entailing the "end of a civilization." This kind of analysis seemed unduly apocalyptic to him. Ten years later, however, in his *In Defense of Decadent Europe*, Aron freely spoke of the May events as inaugurating a "crisis of civilization," a systematic assault on all those authoritative institutions (e.g., the Church, the army, the university) that were necessary to sustain a free and civilized human order. But rather than seeing May '68 as the founding moment of authentic democracy, Aron saw it as a profound "corruption" of the democratic principle.

This pregnant line of argument has been developed by Dominique Schnapper, the distinguished French sociologist and long-

101

time member of the French Constitutional Council (who is also Raymond Aron's daughter). She writes suggestively about a "philosophy of in-distinction" that has become widespread in the Western democratic world. The democratic principle of human and civic equality has been radicalized, as Tocqueville predicted, into a *passion for equality* that perceives "every distinction . . . as discriminatory, every difference as inegalitarian, every inequality as inequitable." The relations between civic equals which is at the heart of democratic political life becomes the unchallenged model for *all* human relations. Moreover, a laudable respect for the accomplishments of different cultures has given way to an absolute relativism that denies the very idea of universal moral judgments and a universal human nature. Such "extreme equality," as Montesquieu already called it in Book 8 of *The Spirit of the Laws*, is a corruption of democracy lurking at the heart of the "democratic" eruption that characterized May 1968.[3]

THE REVOLUTION CONTINUES

The problem confronting the West today is that this corruption or radicalization of democracy is too often confused with democracy itself. In his magisterial *Tocqueville and the Nature of Democracy*, cited in the opening chapter of this book, Pierre Manent refers to democracy's "immoderate friends," who are also its worst enemies. They are its enemies because they undermine the distinctions necessary to preserve democracy's moral health and political vigor. In France today, a new intellectual industry has arisen dedicated to safeguarding the ideological legacy of 1968. The partisans of "humanitarian democracy" vehemently denounce critics of 1968 and its legacy as "reactionaries," even as they deny there is any discernable "*pensée de 68*." A recent book by Serge Audier, for example, expresses venomous disdain for "la pensée anti-68" even as it tries to save Aron (although only half-heartedly) for the camp of "progress"! The important thing, its author tells us, is to recognize 1968 as a "precious moment," the founding moment of a democracy that broke down authoritarian mores, liberated social energies, and defended citizenship in its new meaning as "participation." The old historicist appeal to the camps of "progress" and "reaction" lives on. But now everything stands or falls not with one's judgment of the Soviet Union, the homeland of socialism, but with one's commitment to the memory—and the values—of 1968. Somehow, I do not see decisive progress.

The censorious response of the ideological guardians of 1968 to the slightest criticism of their moral authority reflects one of the most salient features of that event: it undermined the moral and intellectual continuity of Western civilization. The partisans of 1968 date the birth of a European democracy worthy of the name—humanitarian, open, postnational, and postreligious—to the social upheavals of the late 1960s. The "old West," indeed all the old worlds (as Charles Péguy might put it), whether Christian, republican, or classically liberal, are relegated to a "culpable past." That past is suspect precisely because it recognized the importance of other values than the rights of man and exhibited a now unacceptable toleration of wars, colonialism, social paternalism, and religious authoritarianism. At most, this older liberal and Christian West is given its limited due as the "prehistory" of a self-confident, humanitarian global democracy. More frequently, it is looked at warily as a model to be studiously avoided.

The contemporary West which 1968 has bequeathed to us above all defines itself by its adherence to what it calls "democratic values." For a long time, however, the old and new dispensations, political democracy and older moral traditions and affirmations, coexisted without too much (practical) difficulty. In response to the inhuman totalitarianisms of the Left and the

Right that were the scourge of the twentieth century, churchmen discovered the virtues of liberal constitutionalism and political liberals rediscovered the moral law at the heart of Western civilization. Faced with the totalitarian negation of constitutionalism, the moral law, and the very ideas of unchanging truth and common humanity, liberals and conservatives rallied in support of a West that was still able to draw upon the best of both the modern and the premodern traditions. 1968 shattered this antitotalitarian consensus and gave birth to "postmodern democracy."

The relentless assault on the principle of authority proceeds apace. This process is so regularized that we have ceased to notice or appreciate its truly revolutionary character. Our political orders are bereft of statesmanship, the family is a shell of its former self, and influential currents within the churches no longer know how to differentiate between the sublime demands of Christian charity and demagogic appeals to democratic humanitarianism. Europeans have increasingly severed a legitimate and salutary concern for human rights from its political context, which is self-government within a territorial state indebted to the broad traditions of civilization. They desire what Pierre Manent calls "pure democracy." They increasingly defer to an "idea of democracy" which has no tolerance for the crucial historical, cultural, and political prerequisites of democratic self-government. Nineteen sixty-eight played a central role, as both cause and effect, in this reduction of a capacious tradition of liberty to an idea of democracy committed to a single principle: the maximization of individual autonomy and consent. One of the enduring lessons of May 1968, therefore, is surely that the idea of democracy is never sufficient unto itself. As pure abstraction or ideology, democracy risks becoming a deadly enemy of self-government and of human liberty and dignity, properly understood.

6

Conservatism, Democracy, and Foreign Policy

In a penetrating 1949 essay, the Hungarian political philosopher Aurel Kolnai wrote that in our time, a balanced defense
of liberty should aim "to *displace the spiritual stress* from the
'common man' aspect of Democracy to its aspect of constitutionalism and of moral continuity with the high tradition of Antiq-
uity, Christendom, and the half-surviving Liberal cultures of
yesterday." Kolnai's profoundly conservative appreciation of the
moral foundations of democracy provides a principled ground
for resisting "the culture of repudiation"—the antinomian spirit
that inspired and flowed from 1968—and for making one's way
in the culture wars. Kolnai's thought can also provide inspiration
for a principled and prudent foreign policy that does not confuse
a robust defense of liberty with doctrinaire support for democracy abroad. An early critic of both National Socialism and
Soviet Communism, Kolnai knew that the Western world has
every reason to consider totalitarianism the *summum malum*,
the worst political evil. But a variety of legitimate antitotalitarian political options exist even in a democratic age. In foreign
policy, the intellectual alternatives are not exhausted by a choice
between cultural relativism and a democratic progressivism that
overlooks the fragility of political civilization.

In my view, the West's victory over Soviet Communism is best understood not as a victory for democracy per se—especially not for democracy in its current, postnational and postreligious manifestation—but, rather, as a defeat for the utopian illusion that human beings could somehow live free and dignified lives without property, religion, nations, or politics. The collapse of Soviet Communism was the definitive repudiation of what the Hegelio-Marxist philosopher Alexandre Kojève called "the universal and homogenous state." Kojève believed that by the mid-twentieth century the avant-garde of humanity had put "an end to history," to all world-transforming political or ideological contestation. Henceforth, there would be no politics, only the administration of things, whether by Communist commissars or E.U. bureaucrats. This was history's *inevitable* denouement. These fantasies ought to have been revealed for what they were by the *annus mirabilis* 1989.

Yet such is the hold of historicism that politicians and theorists across the ideological spectrum succumbed to the temptation to give a "progressivist" interpretation of the end of the Cold War. Marvelously mirroring Marxist arguments, lifelong anti-Communists now claimed that it was the West's victory in the Cold War that had been inevitable, that Communism was destined to collapse because it had been "on the wrong side of History." In his address to the British parliament in 1982, Ronald Reagan had stated that "the Soviet Union . . . runs against the tide of history by denying freedom and human dignity to its citizens." Surely this noble statesman was correct that Communism entailed nothing less than a fundamental assault on "the natural order of things." But it was another matter to turn the tables on the Marxists by claiming that "History" favored the universal triumph of the democratic ideal. With the systematic breakdown of classical and Christian education in the Western world, few were still capable of articulating an older wisdom that refused to identify the Good with the alleged movement of History.

With the publication of Francis Fukuyama's article "The End of History?" in the *National Interest* in 1989 (and the book which quickly followed on its heels), the world was treated to a sophisticated neo-Marxist interpretation of the fall of Communism, this time at the service of a broadly conservative politics. According to Fukuyama, the end of the Cold War had indeed culminated in something like the "universal and homogenous state." But in one of those displays of dialectical cleverness beloved by social theorists, democratic capitalism was now said to alone embody the authentic "recognition of man by man." In a "Ruse of Reason" worthy of Hegel himself, History had vindicated the bourgeois order whose doom had been prophesied by a century and a half of progressive thought.

Fukuyama's thesis gave powerful impetus to what can be called the "second neoconservatism," an intellectual current that wished to follow up the defeat of Communism with vigorous support for a "global democratic revolution" aided and sustained by the military and political power of the United States. The first neoconservatism, in contrast to the second, had been more anti-totalitarian than democratic in orientation, and was perfectly willing to acknowledge the sheer intractability of cultures and civilizations. Whatever the intellectual pedigree of some of its adherents, the new neoconservatism owed more to Alexandre Kojève than to Leo Strauss, who had been an unremitting critic of the "universal and homogenous state" in all its forms. The new neoconservatism shared few of the older neoconservatism's concerns about the pernicious spiritual and cultural effects of a fully democratized polity and culture (see almost any essay by Irving Kristol from the 1970s) or its hesitations about dogmatic support for human rights in foreign policy (the locus classicus of this position is Jeane J. Kirkpatrick's important 1979 *Commentary* essay, "Dictatorships and Double Standards").

107

FUKUYAMA'S INDICTMENT

In *America at the Crossroads: Democracy, Power, and the Neoconservative Legacy* (2006), Fukuyama ignores his own role in the genesis of the "second neoconservatism." In important respects, the present-day partisans of "muscular Wilsonianism" have built upon Fukuyaman premises about "the end of history" and the unchallenged ideological ascendancy of liberal democracy, even if they have emphasized the efficacy of military power more than Fukuyama now thinks prudent. In his current self-presentation, Fukuyama plays Marx (or a latter-day Menshevik) to William Kristol's Lenin. He defends the desirability and ultimate inevitability of global democratization while criticizing ill-advised efforts to push the process along. He sees himself as the true neoconservative, one who has remained faithful to neoconservatism's original critique of large-scale social engineering and its salutary concern about the unintended consequences of social action. In *America at the Crossroads* and in the postscript to the 2006 edition of *The End of History and the Last Man*, Fukuyama defends a relatively uncontroversial version of modernization theory that owes more to Tocqueville and Weber than to Kojève. He claims that he "never posited a strong version of modernization theory, with rigid stages of development or economically determined outcomes. Contingency, leadership, and ideas always play a complicating role, which made major setbacks possible if not likely."

There is an element of truth in these formulations. The second neoconservatism is more activist than anything suggested in Fukuyama's original speculations about the nature of the post–Cold War world. But just as Leninist voluntarism—the revolutionary effort to give History a shove toward its ultimate destination—was a natural consequence of Marx's own philoso-

108

phy of history, so Fukuyama's announcement of the ideological triumph of liberal democracy was bound to provide inspiration for what was to become the second neoconservatism. Fukuyama cannot evade responsibility for his decisive role in interpreting the collapse of Communism in an essentially progressivist or historicist light. It is also difficult to understand why Fukuyama needed to resort to an obscure mélange of Hegel and Kojève, or to rhetoric about the "end of history," if all he had in mind from the beginning was a relatively innocuous version of modernization theory. This born-again Tocquevillian now more carefully distinguishes between economic and social modernization (which indeed has something "irresistible" about it) and political liberty, which can never simply be guaranteed by unfolding historical or social processes. To make that distinction, however, is to deny any *essential* identification of modernization with "the end of history." It is to affirm with Tocqueville and the classics that the political problem is in principle unsolvable, that History can never substitute for the imperative for human beings "to put reasons and actions in common," as Aristotle put it.

In addition to his failure to appreciate the logic of his own position, Fukuyama's attribution of real or even metaphorical Leninism both to the Bush administration and to contemporary neoconservatives is unjust and irresponsible. It muddies the theoretical waters while adding nothing to our understanding of the real alternatives facing citizens and statesmen today. Leninism entailed a self-conscious abrogation of the moral law in the name of a revolutionary project to create a New Man and a New Society. It was a manifestation of an inhuman ideological impulse that Edmund Burke did not hesitate to call (in different historical circumstances) "metaphysical madness." Leninism inevitably gave rise to totalitarianism because its ends were *contra naturum* and because it provided ideological justification for tyranny and terror on a truly unprecedented scale. Neoconservatives such as

William Kristol may overstate the universal appeal of "democracy" and the role that American power can play in promoting it around the world. That is surely a question for debate and discussion. But they are decent men who have never claimed that moral considerations can be suspended in pursuit of utopian ends.

Moreover, the neoconservatives are wrestling with a real problem made more pressing by the terrorist attacks of September 11, 2001—namely, the multiple ways in which social stagnation and political authoritarianism conspire to reinforce fanaticism throughout the Arab Islamic world. And however muscular their approach to foreign policy, they have not advocated the indiscriminate use of military power or succumbed to the illusion that democracy can simply be imposed from the barrel of a gun. To suggest otherwise is to engage in wild caricatures of a serious, if flawed, approach to the conduct of American foreign policy. There is something unhinged about John Gray's suggestion in the pages of the *American Interest* (Summer 2006) that neoconservatism represents the continuation of the Marxist-Leninist project and that it will inevitably lead to the same tragic consequences. These extreme formulations—worthy of an ideologue and not a political philosopher—would be easy to dismiss if they did not also recur with alarming regularity in realist and paleoconservative criticisms of neoconservatism in general, and the Bush foreign policy in particular. President Bush was the first conservative president to be regularly castigated as a "Jacobin" and "Leninist" by a significant number of critics within the conservative intellectual community. Such criticisms paradoxically obscured the genuine weaknesses of the Bush Doctrine by attributing mere fanaticism to a foreign policy that in truth had equal measures of strength and weakness.

A Neoconservative Foreign Policy?

President Bush's critics tended to presuppose that the Bush administration was carrying out a plan of action that was designed in advance by neoconservative intellectuals. In this view, President Bush was somehow a captive of a cabal of ex-leftist Jewish intellectuals, students of Leo Strauss, and a group of writers and thinkers around William Kristol's *Weekly Standard*. It was conveniently forgotten or ignored that none of the principals in the administration was a neoconservative—with the arguable exception of Vice President Cheney, who indeed moved closer to neoconservative positions during his tenure at the American Enterprise Institute in the 1990s. It must be remembered that neoconservative advocates of a militarily assertive neo-Wilsonian foreign policy were initially wary of George W. Bush and tended to support the internationalist John McCain in the 2000 Republican primaries. As a candidate, Bush repeatedly expressed his suspicion of humanitarian interventions abroad and called for greater "humility" in the conduct of American foreign policy. The first eight months of the Bush presidency were dedicated to a domestic agenda of "compassionate conservatism" centered around education reform and "faith-based initiatives." Bush's initial instincts about foreign policy—he did not articulate anything as systematic as a doctrine or a grand strategy—were undoubtedly unilateralist, but they were by no means unduly interventionist. In this regard at least, 9/11 did indeed "change everything."

Bush never became a neoconservative—he operates too much on an instinctual plane to join an intellectual party of any sort—but he formed a tactical alliance with those who provided a theoretical rationale for a more assertive foreign policy. The so-called Bush Doctrine "called for offensive operations, including preemptive war, against terrorists and their abetters, more specifically, against the regimes that had sponsored, encouraged, or merely tolerated, any 'terrorist group of global reach.'"[1] If preemptive action (not necessarily of a military sort) against terror-supporting "rogue states" was the weapon of choice of the new strategic doctrine, the promotion of democratic "regime change" provided the moral compass for a foreign policy that aimed to take the fight to an unscrupulous and nihilistic enemy. Its proponents vigorously defended support for democratic transformation in the Middle East as a new kind of realism rather than an ideological crusade motivated by abstract or utopian considerations. This overall project is informed by a strong dose of realism and contains no small element of daring and moral nobility. For too long the United States coddled corrupt, autocratic regimes in the Middle East as long as they kept the oil flowing or served our strategic interests. The new approach provided a comprehensive framework for navigating the post–9/11 world and a sense of mission to an America that had been awakened from her somnolence by the surprise assault on our national soil. President Bush was no doubt inspired by the idea of striking at the very sources of tyranny and terror in the Arab Islamic world. But his decency and respect for common humanity, undeniable virtues in a democratic statesman, led him to exaggerate the prospects for self-government in a region where secular and religious authoritarianism too often compete to shape the destiny of peoples. In addition, President Bush is a moralist who clearly relishes an unequivocal confrontation with political evil. He is inclined to see any qualification of doctrinaire universalism as a choice for "relativism" rather than a salutary recognition of the undeniable fact that self-government has crucial historical, moral, cultural, and spiritual prerequisites.

STRENGTHS AND LIMITS OF POST-9/11 FOREIGN POLICY

The Bush administration was not wrong to recognize important parallels between Jihadist radicalism and the political religions of the twentieth century. Whatever the differences between the "pious cruelty" of the Islamists and the atheistic tyrannies of the twentieth century, both ideological currents disdained bourgeois democracy and repudiated the moral law in the name of ostensibly more sublime aspirations and goals. In *America at the Crossroads*, however, Fukuyama rightfully questions whether Islamism poses the same kind of "existential threat" to Western civilization that was posed by Communism and Nazism. With its open contempt for rationality, civil society, and ordinary morality, and its disdain for less virulent currents of Islam, Jihadist extremism mainly appeals to the marginal and dislocated, to those who have been uprooted by the whirlwinds of globalization. It will never attract the sympathy of Western intellectuals as Communism did during the long social crisis that dominated the first half of the twentieth century. The West must prepare itself for a protracted struggle with a fanatical international movement that aspires to force the whole of humanity to live within "the house of Islam." With such a movement there can be no compromise or negotiated settlement. Still, it is difficult to argue that in this struggle the West's very existence—or the moral legitimacy of liberal democracy—is genuinely at stake.

Any adequate response to the terrorist threat demands a mixture of civic and martial fortitude and political dexterity that goes far beyond the anemic police measures favored by quasi-pacifistic Europeans today. But inexact talk about an open-ended "war on terror"—which implies war without end—does not adequately convey the unsettling gray zone between war and peace that will characterize the international situation for the foreseeable future.* Nor is it self-evident that democracy, especially electoral democracy, can provide the antidote to the Islamist virus.

After 9/11 the Bush administration lost an opportunity to articulate a textured antitotalitarianism on the model of the old neoconservatism, one that combined principled opposition to despotism with a carefully calibrated politics of prudence. Instead, President Bush increasingly defined the global political alternatives in a starkly Manichean way as a choice between democracy and tyranny. His understanding of the contemporary world rested on a doctrinaire political science that recognized one and only one path to human freedom and flourishing. This was the downside of a positive feature. Bush's clear-sighted recognition of Good and Evil was the major source of his principled tough-mindedness as a statesman. He is to be applauded for his ability to forthrightly name the enemy (and to recognize that the West continues to confront deadly enemies) in a democratic world that is increasingly prone to take for granted the spiritual unity of the human race.** But this admirable clarity about the

---

* By the middle of President Bush's second term, senior administration officials sought to replace talk about a "Global War on Terror" with the awkward if perhaps more accurate locution "Global Struggle Against Violent Extremism" (but notice the unwillingness to speak directly about Jihadism or political Islam). The Obama administration has gone even further and has directed its personnel to speak not of an ongoing "struggle" against violent extremism but of an ill-defined "Overseas Contingency Operation," a term which manages to be tepid and Orwellian at the same time. The initial failure to adequately describe the situation confronting America after 9/11 has led to a systematic erosion of intellectual and moral clarity.

** Contrast this with President Obama's tendency to treat international conflict as an unfortunate byproduct of misunderstanding or miscommunication or as a predictable reaction to the heavy-handed policies of his predecessor. If President Bush sometimes erred on the side of Manicheanism, President Obama is too quick to assume Western (and particularly American) "guilt" when addressing the sources of international conflict. But see Obama's Nobel Peace Prize speech of

moral dimensions of the struggle also led the president to be too dismissive of the gray middle ground that more often than not defines the art of statecraft. Bush and his neoconservative allies paradoxically share no small measure of the humanitarianism that they rightly castigate when it emanates from antipolitical European and American leftist intellectuals.

It should be acknowledged, however, that the Bush administration's instincts and policies were often significantly more prudent than its official rhetoric and doctrine might suggest. The administration was no doubt chastened by the difficulty of pacifying Iraq and of introducing lawful government in a country wracked by tribal passions and sectarian divisions. Through bitter experience, it came to appreciate the profound difficulties entailed in bringing self-government to another people, especially one that has been deeply scarred by despotism and is bereft of a settled national consciousness. The administration surely arrived at a more sober appreciation of the sheer intractability of a part of the world deeply rooted in spiritual sources that are alien to the Western experience. Contrary to what its more fevered critics suggest, it had little stomach for organizing a global democratic imperium or embarking on new "wars of choice." While the administration continued to put too much emphasis on the centrality of electoral democracy, it knew how to work with authoritarian allies who oppose Islamist fanaticism or who, in its judgment, provide the best hope for political stability and gradual liberalization.

December 10, 2009, where he defends the notion of "just war" and acknowledges that "there will be times when nations—acting individually or in concert—will find the use of force not only necessary but morally justified."

CONSERVATISM AND THE RHETORIC OF DEMOCRACY

But the administration's official rhetoric continued to be marred by a tendency to treat modern democracy as a self-evident desideratum, even as the regime "according to nature." As friendly critics such as Fareed Zakaria pointed out, both the administration and its neoconservative allies woefully underestimated the despotic propensities inherent in electoral democracy, and this despite the rising electoral fortunes of Islamist parties such as the Muslim Brotherhood and Hamas in the Middle East and of a leftist authoritarian like Hugo Chavez in Venezuela. They spoke ritualistically about "democracy" when what they must really have had in mind is that complex synthesis of the rule of law, constitutionalism, federalism, and representative government that Zakharia calls "constitutional liberalism." Their democratic monomania marks a break with an older conservative tradition which always insisted that Western liberty draws on intellectual and spiritual resources broader and deeper than that of modern democracy. The idioms of constitutionalism and representative government have little place in a doctrine that places such inordinate emphasis on the love of liberty in the human soul and its natural expression through majority votes.

Critics who raised perfectly legitimate and necessary questions about the cultural prerequisites of democratic self-government were summarily dismissed by President Bush or Prime Minister Blair as cultural relativists, or even as racists—as if democracy arises automatically once impediments are removed. As ominously, the partisans of global democracy turn a blind eye to the historical evidence that suggests it is not from authoritarian regimes, but from weak and fledgling "democracies," that totalitarianism arises: consider Russia in 1917, Italy in 1922, and Germany in 1933.* The best conservative thinkers of the last two centuries have been wary of unalloyed democracy precisely because they cared deeply about the preservation of human liberty and recognized the powerful affinities between mass democracy and modern totalitarianism. There are totalitarian propensities inherent in what the French political philosopher Bertrand de Jouvenel once called "sovereignty in itself": the illusion that the "sovereign" human will is the ultimate arbiter of the moral and political world.

We were confronted, then, with a foreign policy that in many respects operated within sober parameters of principle and prudence—but which expressed itself in a self-defeating rhetoric that encouraged overreach and left the administration vulnerable to tendentious criticism. When the Bush administration worked with moderate pro-American autocrats such as General Pervez Musharraf in Pakistan it was inevitably accused of hypocrisy. Putting inordinate stress on the necessity of building *democracy* in Iraq and Afghanistan—rather than speaking more modestly about strengthening lawful and representative institutions in both countries—created unreasonable expectations that were bound to be disappointed. Such democracy rhetoric also disarms legitimate concerns about religious extremism (e.g., the imposition of *Sharia*) when it is legitimized through the electoral process. Who are we to challenge the sovereignty of a *democratic* people? A more calibrated rhetoric, one that emphasizes the need to gradually introduce lawful and nondespotic political orders in countries ravaged by despotism or beset by corruption and authoritarianism, would be less dramatic and perhaps less inspiring. But it would better describe the more modest and often quite realistic hopes that drive actual American policy in countries such as Iraq and Afghanistan.

---

* This point was central to Charles de Gaulle's famous "Bayeux address" of June 16, 1946.

Excessively doctrinaire rhetoric about democracy also creates misplaced pressures to confront nontotalitarian regimes, such as Vladimir Putin's and Dmitri Medvedev's Russia, with demands for "liberalization" that have nothing to do with America's legitimate national interests and everything to do with the view that Western-style liberal democracy provides the *only* legitimate model for political development in our time. This put the Bush administration in a bind. Vice President Cheney followed up a May 4, 2006, speech in Vilnius, Lithuania—one which implicitly threatened Russia with a "color revolution" of its own if it did not move in a more democratic direction—with trips to Kazakhstan and Khirgistan to do business with the local tyrants. Such a brazen act of double-dealing confirms the suspicions of skeptics who are already convinced that American "universalism" is little more than a cover for national egoism and will-to-power. The spirited resistance to tyranny that was the hallmark of Bush administration rhetoric since 9/11 should have been moderated and complemented by a greater awareness of local conditions and a greater modesty about America's capacity to judge—and dictate—the appropriate conditions for self-government abroad. To its credit, the Obama administration has gone some way in this direction, especially in its policy toward Russia, even as it has been too hesitant to support a resurgent civil society against anti-American theocrats in Iran. In Russia, "National Bolsheviks" of the most unsavory sort, not Western-style liberals, are perhaps the real alternative to Putin's moderately authoritarian if comparatively liberal regime.

The vituperative exchanges between neoconservatives and paleoconservatives, and between foreign policy "realists" and "idealists," did little to contribute to the articulation of a politics of prudence worthy of the name. The full array of American conservative intellectuals and politicians needs to learn how to judiciously combine spiritedness and moderation, Churchillian fortitude and prudent self-restraint, in a way that does justice to the perils that stem from both too much and too little national self-assertion. The excesses of the Obama administration—in particular its excessively apologetic foreign policy—in no way justify a failure to come to terms with the lessons to be learned from the mistakes of Bush-era foreign policy.

THE SECOND INAUGURAL:
NATURE, HISTORY, AND THE HUMAN SOUL

The democratic universalism of the Bush Doctrine was expressed with particular lucidity in the Second Inaugural Address delivered by the president on January 21, 2005. That speech is the best single articulation of the moral and philosophical premises underlying President Bush's foreign policy—or at least of the official doctrine that animated it. But it also reveals some of the deeply problematic assumptions informing the Bush administration's policy "to seek and support the growth of democratic movements and institutions in every nation and culture, with the ultimate goal of ending tyranny in our world." That heady goal was presented as a fully practical ideal even if Bush conceded on that occasion that it is likely to be the "concentrated work of generations." That perfunctory concession to gradualism in no way qualified the president's "complete confidence in the eventual triumph of freedom" or his belief that democracy, and democracy alone, is the regime that most fully coheres with the nature and needs of human beings. For President Bush, democracy has the support of the deepest longings of the human soul and of a Providential God who is also the "Author of Liberty."

In his Second Inaugural, President Bush acknowledges that democracy can take a variety of local or cultural expressions. He denies that the United States has any interest in "impos(ing) our

119

own style of government on the unwilling." Still, he fully identifies democracy as a political form with the imperative of self-government. Whatever latitude is left to citizens and statesmen has
to do with the kind of democracy that will protect human rights
and human dignity within particular historical or cultural set-
tings. President Bush implicitly affirms that the whole of humanity should and will eventually live under the liberal democratic
dispensation. To that extent at least, he and his speechwriters
share the Kojèvean-Fukuyaman premise that the "mutual recognition" of man by man will inevitably culminate in a "universal
and homogenous state."

In the Second Inaugural, Bush speaks grandiloquently
about "the global appeal of liberty" and makes no distinction
between support for liberty and the promotion of a rather ill-
defined "democracy." The president simply ignores or disregards
everything in modern historical experience that suggests that
modernization is compatible with various forms of "democratic
despotism." The defeat of Communism is interpreted as definitive
proof that "the world is moving toward liberty," since "the call of
freedom comes to every mind and every soul."

In his remarks to the people of Hungary delivered on June 22,
2006, to commemorate the fiftieth anniversary of the Hungarian
Revolution, President Bush makes a similar claim that "the desire
for liberty is universal, because it is written by our Creator into
the hearts of every man, woman, and child on the Earth." In this
speech, Bush pays eloquent tribute to the noble struggle of Hungarians in 1956, all the while treating that "anti-totalitarian revolution" (as Raymond Aron called it at the time), that collective
revolt against the ideological "lie," as evidence of the inevitable
triumph of democracy over "dictatorship." In doing so, however,
he risks rendering that great event banal by turning it into one
more illustration of the Whig version of history—the view that
all events in the past are a preparation for the development and

diffusion of Western-style constitutionalism. The specificity of Communist totalitarianism, the Christian and European character of the Hungarian people, and the fact that Hungarians themselves took the initiative to restore their national independence and the authentic meaning of words are all overlooked in this rendering of events. The Hungarian Revolution instead becomes raw material for the inevitable victory of democracy in every time and place.

As hortatory rhetoric, the president's words are undoubtedly stirring and even ennobling. As political reflection, they reveal a shallow understanding of the complex passions, interests, and motives that move human beings. President Bush dogmatically presupposes that love of liberty is the predominant, even the overarching motive of the human soul. He not only downplays the cultural prerequisites of ordered liberty or democratic self-government but also abstracts from the sempiternal drama of good and evil in each and every human soul. The president's unqualified universalism abstracts from the fact that hatred of despotism by no means automatically translates into love of liberty or a settled and disciplined capacity for self-government. It ignores Tocqueville's profound insight, luminously expressed in *The Old Regime and the Revolution*, that the pure love of liberty—the passion for political freedom and of "government of God and the laws alone"—is a "sublime taste" reserved for a few souls and incomprehensible to "mediocre" ones.

Bush sometimes recurs to the best conservative wisdom and acknowledges that self-government necessarily entails "the governing of the self." He rightly asserts that human rights are "ennobled by service, and mercy." But he more characteristically makes extravagant claims about love of liberty being the incontestable motive of thinking and acting man. As Charles Kesler observed at the time, Bush ignores the palpable fact that while "'people everywhere prefer freedom to slavery' . . . many people everywhere and at all times have been quite happy to enjoy their freedom and all the benefits of someone else's slavery." Self-government is a disposition of the soul that finds powerful support in the soul's refusal to be tyrannized by others. But the two are not equivalent. President Bush is not wrong when he argues that despotism violates the moral law and mutilates the wellsprings of the human spirit. However, he is too quick to identify human nature with a single overarching impulse or desire, and he goes too far in conflating the ways of Providence with the empire of democratic liberty.

Near the end of the Second Inaugural, Bush anticipates some of these criticisms. While continuing to express "complete confidence in the eventual triumph of freedom," he attempts to distance himself from arguments about historical inevitability. "History" by itself determines nothing. Instead, our confidence in the universal triumph of liberty must be rooted in the fact that freedom is the "permanent hope of mankind" and the most powerful "longing of the soul." These poetic invocations do not adequately take into account the decidedly mixed character of human nature. The president should not have been expected, of course, to speak with the precision of a political philosopher. Still, this president of deep Christian conviction paradoxically showed little appreciation for the tragic dimensions of history and the pernicious and permanent effects of original sin on individual and collective life.

HUMANITARIAN DEMOCRACY
VERSUS THE UNITED STATES

Moreover, the reduction of the political problem to the categorical imperative of promoting democracy abroad left the administration and the country vulnerable to those on the Left who identify democracy with a project to emancipate human beings from traditional cultural, moral, and even political restraints. For the partisans of "postmodern" or "humanitarian" democracy, the United States falls far short of the democratic ideal. As Pierre Manent has recently written, European elites "are trying to separate their democratic virtue from all their other characteristics," such as tradition, religion, and especially from the political framework of the nation-state.* They have succumbed to what might be called the "postpolitical temptation." At the same time, "Americans seem more than ever willing—and this disposition extends well beyond the partisans of the current [Bush] administration—to identify everything they do and everything they are with democracy, as such."[2] But what is to prevent the partisans of humanitarian democracy from denying the democratic bona fides of a self-governing people that remains attached to national sovereignty and still acknowledges the importance of traditional arrangements to a regime of self-government? By validating democracy as the *alpha* and *omega* of politics in our time, the Bush Doctrine left America vulnerable to delegitimization at the hands of more radical and "consistent" forms of democratic affirmation. In any case, deference to humanizing universal moral and political truths in no way means that any particular country gives humanity *unmediated access* to the universal. Abraham Lincoln, the noble poet-statesman of the American experiment, beautifully captured this tension when he spoke of Americans as an "almost-chosen people." The United States (and the Western world in general) would cease to be true to itself if it repudiated the universality of its principles. But America surely also

---

* President Obama mirrored these European tendencies in his remarks to the Muslim world in Cairo on June 4, 2009, when he emphatically denied that the United States was in any way a "Christian nation." In doing so, he implicitly identified America with pure democracy, a regime without any substantive historical, cultural, or spiritual roots.

owes much of its greatness to particular national characteristics, to what Orestes Brownson suggestively called our "providential constitution." Otherwise America is in principle "the world," the prototype of a unified humanity, and is destined to be swallowed up by a global imperium that more fully embodies the democratic aspirations of the whole of mankind.

President Bush may not have been a neoconservative in any narrow political or even ideological sense. But his Second Inaugural Address perfectly mirrors the contradictions at the heart of the second neoconservatism. Like President Bush, neoconservatives are proud defenders of the prerogatives of the United States as a free, independent, and self-governing national community. At the same time, they are deeply suspicious of any other national self-assertion, however moderate or humane, that declines, in Pierre Manent's words, to "identify American democracy with the universal as such." At the rhetorical level at least, the second neoconservatism and the partisans of European humanitarian democracy (as well as Bush's successor as president, preoccupied as he is with global public opinion) ultimately differ more about means than ends. They are *frères-ennemis* who promote two distinct paths to the same destination, the "universal and homogenous state."

Neoconservatism's misplaced one-sided emphasis on democracy may be more the rhetorical scaffolding than the heart and soul of neoconservative wisdom. But this democratic monomania acts as an acid, eating away at the coherence of a current of thought whose patriotism, good will, and commitment to the cause of liberty should in no way be doubted. Alas, it cannot provide the basis for a politics of prudence in our time. True conservatism is obliged to be suspicious of the "religion of humanity" in all its forms.

Part IV

Totalitarianism and Terror:
The Dark Underside of Modernity

7

The Totalitarian Subversion of Modernity: Solzhenitsyn on the Self-deification of Man and the Origins of the Modern Crisis

The experience of totalitarianism, that "twentieth-century invention," as Aleksandr Solzhenitsyn once called it, ought to have permanently discredited all facile or naïve progressivism. But as the previous chapter attests, too many in the West mistakenly identified the fall of Communism in East-Central Europe and the Soviet Union with "the overflowing triumph of an all-democratic bliss."[1] The writings of Solzhenitsyn (1918–2008) provide unique resources for understanding both the evils of totalitarianism and the limits of democratic euphoria. Solzhenitsyn was more than a courageous moral witness and a talented and prodigious writer who helped shape the course of history by fatally undermining the moral legitimacy of the Communist enterprise. He was also a historian and philosopher (in the capacious nonacademic sense of the term that is so central to the Russian tradition) who has a great deal to teach us about the totalitarian temptation that shadows—and risks subverting—democratic modernity.

Yet for thirty-five years now, we have lived with the legend of an authoritarian Solzhenitsyn. Without supporting citations, it is said that the Russian Nobel laureate pines for tsarist autocracy, or the creation of an "Orthodox" state, or even for new gulags at the service of an essentially despotic Russian national idea. There is not an iota of evidence to support any of these claims about the greatest antitotalitarian writer of the twentieth century.[2] These slanders can be traced back to the early 1970s, to the confused and angry reaction of left-liberal intellectuals to the publication of such works as *August 1914* (1972), *From Under the Rubble* (1974), and the *Letter to the Soviet Leaders* (1973).

If *August 1914* provided a devastating critique of the sclerotic character of the Russian old regime, of the unwillingness of its purblind bureaucrats and courtiers to adjust thoughtfully to conditions of modernity, it also made clear that Solzhenitsyn had no sympathy for those left-liberals then or in his time who flirted with nihilism, apologized for terrorism, and showed contempt for the best spiritual and cultural traditions of the Russian nation. The luminous essays by Solzhenitsyn and his collaborators in *From Under the Rubble* contemplate a Russian future freed from the evils of ideological despotism. At the same time, its contributors warned against the slavish imitation of the worst features of contemporary Western democracy, including its scientism, subjectivism, and rejection of the classical and Christian resources of the Western tradition.

Of the three aforementioned writings, the *Letter to the Soviet Leaders* was by far the most misunderstood. It is a piece of "esoteric" writing whose call for the Soviet leaders to hold on to power—temporarily—even as they jettison the ideology which provided the only justification for their rule, was nothing less than an invitation for the totalitarian party-state to commit suicide. The *Letter*'s incisive dissection of the theoretical and practical claims of Marxism, its defense of *glasnost* in civic and intellectual life, its searing indictment of collectivization, and its subtle Augustinian defense of freedom—but no special privileges—for religious believers, were all but forgotten in the controversies that followed. Solzhenitsyn's qualified endorsement of a nonideological authoritarianism *during the transition period* from totalitarian dictatorship was widely confused with a *theoretical* endorsement of authoritarian rule.

Solzhenitsyn's numerous explanations of the rhetorical strategy underlying the 1973 *Letter*, as well as his defense of local self-government ("the democracy of small spaces") and the rule of law in such works as 1990's *Rebuilding Russia* and 1998's *Russia in Collapse*, have done little to assuage his critics. As a result, Solzhenitsyn's political ideas are fundamentally misunderstood in the West (and by his "Westernizing" critics in Russia, too). By the time that Solzhenitsyn delivered his friendly if hard-hitting criticisms of aspects of the West in his June 1978 Harvard address, his critics were prepared to filter them through an essentially tendentious interpretive framework. Alas, not nearly enough has changed in that regard over the past thirty years.

The Fragility of Modern Liberty

Solzhenitsyn, though, remains what he has always been—an eloquent and principled defender of liberty and human dignity.* Yet Solzhenitsyn is acutely aware of the fragility of the Enlightenment principles that undergird the regime of modern liberty. In contradistinction to the dominant current of the age, he rejects the idea of "pluralism" as an "autonomous principle," an end in itself, rather than an essential means for pursuing a truth that imperfect human beings perceive all too often through a glass darkly. Solzhenitsyn's refusal to sever freedom from an order of truth sets him apart from every radically modern articulation of human liberty and makes him suspicious in the eyes of those

---

* The distinguished Russianist John Dunlop has suggestively described *The Gulag Archipelago* as a "personalistic feast" that pays tribute to the many faces of individual personality and conscience that refused to give way before the ideological deformation of reality.

who identify liberty with the rejection of all natural or divine limits. If the immediate target of works such as *In the First Circle* and *The Gulag Archipelago* was the soul-destroying mendacity of an ideological regime that tried to remake men and societies at a stroke, these works *ultimately* point toward a more fundamental engagement with the limits of the philosophy of the Enlightenment and of the secular anthropocentrism that is at its core.

Solzhenitsyn remarked in an interview with German novelist Daniel Kehlmann (*Le Figaro*, December 1, 2006) that the "global consequences" of the "collapse" of anthropocentrism in the twentieth century have not yet become fully apparent. But in four capital texts—the 1978 Harvard address, a 1979 BBC interview with Janis Sapiets, a December 2000 address to the French Academy of Moral and Political Sciences on the occasion of receiving its Grand Prize, and in key chapters of his multivolume masterwork *The Red Wheel*—Solzhenitsyn has provided a suggestive critique of the political and social doctrine that he calls "rationalistic humanism" or "anthropocentricity." Solzhenitsyn also gives an account of the concrete ways in which the principles of theoretical modernity have left decent political orders vulnerable to moral, political, and cultural subversion from within and to hostile forces from without. Solzhenitsyn's analysis has been mistaken for a systematic rejection of the modern world or as evidence of a lack of commitment to political liberty. But as the political theorist Delba Winthrop pointed out in a seminal article written nearly thirty years ago, in his Harvard address Solzhenitsyn criticized America not for its "love of freedom," a love that he shared, but for its increasing inability to defend freedom "against materialism." Winthrop accurately summarizes Solzhenitsyn's position: "If freedom is to be defended against materialism, freedom must have a meaning and end other than material well-being." And she tellingly adds, "It is for the failure to help us see this that Solzhenitsyn criticized the fundamental principles of modernity."

The Limits of "Anthropocentric Humanism"

In the Harvard address, Solzhenitsyn defines anthropocentric humanism as "the proclaimed and practiced autonomy of man from any higher force above him." Solzhenitsyn's true alternative to "anthropocentricity" has nothing to do with theocracy. In fact, in the same text Solzhenitsyn notes (and he reiterates the point) that "the Middle Ages had come to a natural end by exhaustion, having become an intolerable despotic repression of man's physical nature in favor of the spiritual one." He calls not for a return to a past which is in any case unavailable and undesirable, but for an "ascension" to the "next anthropological stage," "where our physical nature will not be cursed, as in the Middle Ages, but even more importantly, our spiritual being will not be trampled upon, as in the Modern Era."

Following such conservative liberals as Alexis de Tocqueville or François Guizot in the nineteenth century, or in the manner of the best antitotalitarian reflection of the twentieth century, Solzhenitsyn calls for a renewed recognition and appreciation of the limits of any political project built upon the problematic foundations of the human will. Like his predecessors, Solzhenitsyn forthrightly rejects "the self-sovereignty of man." In response to this seeming reduction of modernity to anthropocentricity, one is tempted to accuse Solzhenitsyn of painting with too broad a brush. But as Pierre Manent pointed out in his 1993 essay "Christianity and Democracy," "the history of modern philosophy, from Machiavelli to Nietzsche, appears as oriented to and animated by the elaboration of the concept of the will." In its most radical forms, the "unbridled affirmation of the human will" is joined to "the unlimited polemic against Christianity." The philosophical architects of modernity such as Bacon and Descartes identified the task of philosophy with nothing less audacious than making human beings "the masters and possessors of nature." In *Leviathan* (1651), Thomas Hobbes explicitly denied that there are any superintending principles of justice above the human will: "Justice and propriety begin with the constitution of [the] commonwealth." To be sure, Solzhenitsyn recognizes that statesmen such as the American founding fathers often deferred to older and richer religious and philosophical traditions predating the anthropocentric emphasis of modernity. This was a great source of vitality for modern liberal regimes. But at the heart of the modern affirmation of the "rights of man," however salutary it may have been in the struggle against despotism, is an implied rejection of the sovereignty of both nature and God, of any authority outside of the human will.

Anthropocentric humanism culminates not in true freedom but in the monstrous self-deification of man, and in the willful denial of a "Supreme Complete Entity" that "restrain(s) our passions and irresponsibility." A humanism shorn of gratitude for the givenness of things tends to deny "the existence of intrinsic evil in man," writes Solzhenitsyn and will succumb to "the dangerous trend of worshiping man and his material needs." Solzhenitsyn's alternative to modern willfulness, as we have seen, is not a return to coercive authoritarianism. Rather, he calls for "voluntary self-limitation." Such self-limitation rejects the "total emancipation" from "the moral heritage of Christian centuries with their great reserves of mercy and sacrifice" that is characteristic of radical modernity. The illusion of radical modernity that such emancipation can give rise to anything but a coarsening of the human soul, and in the worst cases to the triumph of Radical Evil, has been the twentieth century's sad privilege to explode.

THE MODERN CRISIS AND AN "UNEXPECTED KINSHIP"

In the manner familiar to readers of conservative-minded political philosophers such as Leo Strauss and Eric Voegelin, Solzhenitsyn asserts that the erosion of the moral capital of the premodern world has given rise to a "harsh spiritual crisis and a political impasse." "All the celebrated technological achievements of progress, including the conquest of outer space, do not redeem the twentieth century's moral poverty, which no one could have imagined even as late as the nineteenth century," he writes in the Harvard address. According to Solzhenitsyn, one source and manifestation of this "crisis" is the "unexpected kinship" that has been manifested between moderate forms of humanism and more radical and consistent forms of modern materialism. Once liberalism—and socialism—succumbed to "freedom from religion and religious responsibility"—to the full practical consequences of anthropocentricity—they were vulnerable to that "current of materialism which is farthest to the left." The current of materialism that is "most consistent, always proves to be stronger, more attractive, and victorious." Solzhenitsyn believes that the underlying "kinship" between every form of modern humanism helps explain the "enthusiastic support" that an "enormous number of Western intellectuals" gave to Communism by denying, justifying, or explaining away its crimes. Solzhenitsyn says in the Harvard address that they "felt the kinship!" and lost the capacity to resolutely oppose the depredations of Communism.

Solzhenitsyn develops this point more pungently in the remarks that he delivered to the French Academy of Moral and Political Sciences in December 2000:

> Let us go back to the 1920s and the 1930s. The best minds of
> Europe were full of admiration for communist totalitarian-

ism. They were unstinting in their praise for it, joyfully put themselves at its service, lent it their names, their signatures and attended its meetings. How could this have happened? Shouldn't these wise men have been able to see through the aggressive wave of Bolshevik propaganda? During that period, as I well remember, the Bolsheviks were loudly proclaiming, "We communists are the only true humanists." No, these eminent intellectuals were not blind, but carried away by the mere sound of communist ideas since they felt and were aware of their common genetic ties to them. The common roots of liberalism, socialism, and communism go back to the century of enlightenment. That is why, in all countries without exception, the socialists have failed to show any firmness in dealing with the communists. With good reason, they have looked upon them as "first cousins"—or at least as "second cousins." The liberals for the same reason, have always shown themselves weak-kneed in facing communism. They also have common ideological and secular roots.[3]

Solzhenitsyn may overstate his case. The Enlightenment was more variegated than he suggests and not all its currents succumbed to atheistic fanaticism. In its more moderate Anglo-American currents, Enlightenment thought oscillated between residual and real respect for the moral law and a more radical commitment to "liberation" from what Jefferson famously called "monkish ignorance and superstition." In addition, there were honorable liberals and socialists who stood up to totalitarian mendacity and criminality. Beacons of truth and decency like George Orwell and Sidney Hook come to mind. But Solzhenitsyn is surely right that many leftist intellectuals succumbed to the totalitarian temptation precisely because they had no principled ground for resisting it. Sharing many of the aspirations and goals of Communism, including its desire for complete emancipation from the moral heritage of the Western tradition, they turned a blind eye to evil committed at the service of ostensibly "progressive" ends or goals. They gave in to the chief moral debility of the intellectual in modern times: the illusion that "there are no enemies to the Left." The story has been ably (if depressingly) chronicled in Paul Hollander's *Political Pilgrims* (1980) and analyzed with force and precision in Raymond Aron's classic 1955 work, *The Opium of the Intellectuals.*

TRUE AND FALSE LIBERALS

The examination of the "self-weakening and capitulation" (as Solzhenitsyn put it in the 1979 BBC interview) of Russia's liberals and socialists to the hard or totalitarian Left is also one of the principal themes of *The Red Wheel*. This multivolume work is Solzhenitsyn's magisterial literary-historical account of the events leading up to the Bolshevik revolution of 1917. Unlike most liberals in Russia and the West today, Solzhenitsyn sees the February revolution of 1917 as an unmitigated disaster rather than the dawn of a regretfully short-lived Russian democracy. The first Russian revolution of 1917 undermined whatever prospects Russia had for the gradual development and consolidation of lawful constitutional government. The determined efforts of Pyotr Stolypin, prime minister of Russia from 1906 to 1911 and the last great statesman of the old regime, to create a solid class of citizen-proprietors were undone by the land seizures, anarchy, and conflagrations that overtook the countryside in 1917. The liberal statesmen who came to power as a result of the first Russian revolution of 1917 were fully convinced of their superiority to the tsar's ministers, including Stolypin (for whom they had nothing but contempt). But as Solzhenitsyn told Janis Sapiets in

1979, "they turned out to be a collection of spineless mediocrities, who let things slide rapidly into Bolshevism."

From the very first day, the Provisional Government formed by the leaders of the old Left opposition in the Duma was incapable of governing. As Solzhenitsyn puts it in the same interview, "the Provisional Government actually existed, mathematically speaking, for minus two days; in other words, it completely lost control two days before it was set up." Solzhenitsyn's objection is not to the revolutionaries' aspiration for civic and political freedom, an aspiration he shares. But as he shows in chapter 7 of *November 1916* ("Origin of the Kadets"), the dominant current of Russian liberalism was not so liberal after all. The main spokesmen for Russian liberalism refused to act as honest brokers between the state and Russian society. They rejected reasonable initiatives from the state and displayed a shameless indulgence toward revolutionary extremism and terrorism. Russia's Constitutional Democrats, or "Kadets," as they were popularly called, developed out of the *zemstvo* movement of local assemblies in the period immediately before the revolution of 1905. But instead of resting content with a consultative role within a multitiered constitutional order, they agitated for the immediate granting of a Western-style constitution. And once a constitutional order was established in October 1905, they did their best to subvert it in the name of thoroughgoing revolutionary transformation.

As the conservative *zemstvo* leader D. M. Shipov put it at the time, they made "rights and guarantees" the basis of everything and "frittered away the religious and moral idea which was still intact in the mind of the people." Solzhenitsyn draws some general conclusions about the vulnerability of such "false liberals" to cooptation by the revolutionary and nihilistic Left. His insightful observations on this theme in chapter 7 of *November 1916* are worth quoting at length:

Just as the Coriolis effect is constant over the whole of this earth's surface, and the flow of rivers is deflected in such a way that it is always the right bank that is eroded and crumbles, while the floodwater goes leftward, so do all the forms of democratic liberalism on earth strike always to the right and caress the left. Their sympathies always with the left, their feet are capable of shuffling only leftward, their heads bob busily as they listen to leftist arguments—but they feel disgraced if they take a step to or listen to a word from the right.

"Kadet liberalism," as Solzhenitsyn calls it, is a "false liberalism" incapable of "following a firm line of its own." Its disdain for tradition and authority, its indifference or contempt for religion, its fear of being outmaneuvered on the Left, means that it is incapable of defending "a middle line for social development" against revolutionaries on the Left and reactionaries on the Right. Solzhenitsyn saves the appellation of "true liberal" for those like Stolypin and his fictional Colonel Vorotyntsev, who try to meld tradition and modernity, who know that order and freedom are inseparable, who know how to prudently exercise authority, and who are not afraid of raising the wrath of a militant Left. That Left only knows how to destroy rather than to build anything constructive or durable.

A Revealing Episode

In a powerful chapter of *April 1917* (chapter 27, "Disabled Veterans Demonstrate"), Solzhenitsyn provides a particularly revealing illustration of how Russia's supposedly liberal forces cowered in impotence or displayed limitless indulgence toward the Bolsheviks, and in the end allowed them to seize power almost effortlessly in October 1917. A group of disabled veterans have come to the Tauride Palace in St. Petersburg to protest Lenin's return to Russia and his call for an immediate cessation of hostilities with Germany. Various leaders of the new Russia greet the demonstrators respectfully while chastising them for their spirited denunciations of Lenin. "Comrades, that's not the right way to do things. We have to be tolerant of his views as well; everyone must be at liberty to say whatever he wants to say." The disabled veterans are told that it is necessary to be tolerant of Lenin, even if he is a provocateur or aids the German cause. He is, after all, no counterrevolutionary and thus by definition cannot be an enemy of Russia's new liberal order. Meanwhile, a group of Lenin's supporters begin insulting and manhandling the invalids as they prepare to be transported back to their hospital beds. The disintegration of society was so rapid by the spring of 1917 that no power could be marshaled even for so small a task as protecting Russia's disabled veterans from thuggery on the part of lawless and revolutionary elements. This chapter perfectly illustrates the "self-weakening and capitulation" of a moderate Left that could only see enemies on the Right even as the Bolsheviks prepared for a seizure of total power.

CONCLUSION

Solzhenitsyn believes that the lessons of the February revolution are relevant for Russia and the West today. The precipitous leap into freedom in February 1917 prepared Russia not for democracy—as liberals continue to think today—but for a seventy-year experience of inhuman totalitarianism. The failure of Russians to confront adequately the meaning of the February revolution during the long period of Soviet rule left them vulnerable to the anarchic freedom of the Russian 1990s—a freedom equally disconnected from morality, the rule of law, and genuine self-govern-

ment. "False liberals" once again lost sight of the moral foundations of freedom and the intimate connection between authority
and liberty. For the foreseeable future Russians will be living with
the consequences of this moral and intellectual abdication.

On a deeper philosophical plane, Solzhenitsyn understands
these developments to be multifaceted manifestations of a deeper
crisis provoked by anthropocentric humanism. In the twentieth
century, moderate forms of secular humanism showed a remarkable inability to stand up to the secular religion of Communist
totalitarianism. Today, Solzhenitsyn suggests, "rationalistic
humanism" rests content with "enlightened self-interest" as the
only sure guide for private and public life. But without renewed
respect for the "golden key" of self-limitation, without genuine deference to "the Creator of the Universe," such humanism
promises to be less the basis of "an auspicious and promising glo-
balism" than an invitation to new forms of authoritarianism and
manipulation.* The lesson is clear: the genuine promise of the
modern world cannot be actualized on the basis of the untenable
principles of theoretical modernity.

---

* In this paragraph I have drawn freely from Solzhenitsyn's December 13, 2000,
address to the French Academy of Moral and Political Sciences. The Russian
writer's wise recommendation of "voluntary self-limitation" on that occasion
is marred by hyperbolic references to "an authoritative and universal economic
totalitarianism" allegedly promoted by the forces of economic globalization.
But even Solzhenitsyn concedes that countries "here and there have managed
an economic 'takeoff.'" When those countries include vibrant democracies
such as Taiwan and South Korea and emerging economic powerhouses like
China and India it is surely misplaced to speak about the transformation of a
"humanism of global promise into a humanism by directional control." Nonetheless, Solzhenitsyn is absolutely right to warn against the growing emancipation of economic criteria, however legitimate within their own sphere, from
salutary moral and political control.

8

"Moral Insanity" and "Moral Squalor": Terrorism as a Political and Cultural Phenomenon

Solzhenitsyn sheds much needed light on the self-destructive "kinship" that left-liberal intellectuals sometimes felt for totalitarianism. He brings the genius of a writer and the insights of a historian and moral philosopher to bear on one of the most perplexing and disturbing phenomena of modern times. Working at the intersection of academic and public discourse, the British historian Michael Burleigh provides a quite complementary reflection on the tendency of modern intellectuals to succumb to inhuman abstractions, abstractions that provide an impetus for and justification of tyranny and terror in modern times. Burleigh's work is informed by prodigious learning and is written with a wit, clarity, and energy that sets his books apart from almost all academic writing on history and politics. A specialist on German history, in recent years he has turned his attention to chronicling the "abusive exploitation of the human religious sentiment" (the term is that of the early twentieth-century Italian Catholic statesman and political thinker Luigi Sturzo) by the totalitarian ideologies and political movements of modern times.

Burleigh's *Blood and Rage: A Cultural History of Terrorism*,[1] like his "new history" of *The Third Reich* and his exploration of messianic "political religions" in *Earthly Powers* and *Sacred Causes*, confronts "the bloody crossroads" of modern nihilism and political violence.[2] Those previous works highlighted the multiple ways in which the modern ideological state ("from the Jacobins onward") was "responsible for the most lethal instances of terrorism" in modern times. This volume examines those terrorist organizations and movements who have tried over the past century and a half to "create a psychological climate of fear in order to compensate for the legitimate political power they do not possess." Without ever losing focus on contemporary manifestations of terrorism, this rich and provocative "cultural history of terrorism" goes a long way toward expanding our historical memory and deepening our understanding of the moral and political issues at stake in modern terrorism. One of its most important contributions is to illuminate three nineteenth century political movements—the Irish Fenians, Russian "populists" and nihilists, and the anarchists—who indelibly shaped the theory and practice of modern terrorism.

Without downplaying the importance of "ideas and ideology," Burleigh focuses on "terrorism as a career, a culture, and a way of life." In his view, ideology serves as "a detonator that enables a pre-existing mix to explode." Burleigh has no time of day for those who "harbor a sneaking admiration for those who wish to change the world by violence." He refuses to give undue credence to the excuses and justifications of those who murder with impunity. His emphasis is rightly on the "moral insanity" and "moral squalor" of those who choose terrorism as a way of life. Ably drawing on the insights of Dostoevsky and Joseph Conrad (as he had already done to brilliant effect in *Earthly Powers* and *Sacred Causes*), he shows what happens when human beings transform "abstract grievances" into "hysterical rage": they give way to the urge to destroy the world as it is with all is imperfections but also with its manifold possibilities for improvement and change.

THE FENIANS AND THE ROOTS OF THE IRA

Blood and Rage begins with three chapters ("Green," "Red," "Black") that set the stage for everything that follows (the chapters are named after the color of the flags of the three revolutionary movements under discussion). The first explores terrorism in its "green" form: the "Fenian dynamiters" who tried to provoke a general insurrection in Ireland in the last decades of the nineteenth century. Lacking widespread public support, they unleashed a terror campaign throughout the British Isles. Burleigh freely acknowledges the injustices and oppression that drove Irishmen to armed revolt against the British authorities. But the turn by some Irish nationalists to terror of an increasingly indiscriminate character occurred at a time when Charles Stewart Parnell and other advocates for the Irish cause were amply represented in Parliament and many in the British political class were resigning themselves to the necessity of Irish Home Rule. Whether it was the Crimean War of the 1850s or the "Great War" of 1914–1918, Irish Catholics fought in large numbers and with impressive heroism for the common cause. But extreme nationalists were committed to transforming "British imperial difficulties into Irish opportunities." They were willing to cooperate with enemies of freedom as long as they were also enemies of Great Britain. (This pattern would continue well into the 1970s and 1980s with the Irish Republican Army's active collaboration with and support from such unsavory regimes and movements as Libya, Cuba, the PLO, the Basque ETA, and the Communist dictatorship in Czechoslovakia.)

Burleigh notes the Fenians' almost complete dependence upon Irish emigrés in the United States and Great Britain for financial support and military expertise. He criticizes the United States government for being "culpably indulgent toward Fenian terrorism" by refusing to crack down on the open solicitation of money for what were obviously terrorist fronts (he also bitterly observes that the same turning of a blind eye would persist "for the next hundred years"). When the British government threatened terrorists who were guilty beyond doubt with capital punishment, "progressive celebrities such as Charles Bradlaugh, John Stuart Mill, and Karl Marx" signed petitions demanding a stay of execution. This, too, is a pattern of misplaced sympathy that would repeat itself for the next hundred years throughout the Western world. As Burleigh observes, the Fenians could rely upon the uncritical support of too many in the Irish emigration as well as the tendency of some middle-class intellectuals to romanticize terrorists whose ends were inseparable from their sordid means.

The Fenians were, Burleigh writes, "the historic core of, and the mythologized model for what became the Irish Republican Army." The IRA, too, did everything to "capitalize on Britain's imperial woes," and through the "choreographing" of the "blood sacrifice" which was the Easter Rising of 1916 largely succeeded in creating the mythology of an Irish national movement that was in fact little more than an expression of "rabid Catholic sectarianism." Some of Burleigh's critics have attacked his treatment of the "Irish Question," here and in *Sacred Causes*, as being moved by a particular animus toward the Irish cause. In truth, Burleigh, an English Roman Catholic, excoriates the shameless mythologies of *both* "Unionists" and Irish Republicans. In a later chapter ("Small Nation Terror") he highlights the crude sadism and criminality present among terrorists and their supporters on both sides of the republican and unionist divides.

What Burleigh will not tolerate are historically ungrounded mythologies that lead otherwise intelligent people to show sympathy for ideologues and thugs. While he welcomes the cessation of widespread sectarian violence that has followed the Good Friday agreement of Easter 1998, he argues it has come at a steep price: Northern Ireland is now ruled by a "condominium" of extremist political movements that have ratified the *de facto* sectarian partitioning of Ulster. The peace agreement has left many "republican areas effectively removed from the control of normal courts and policing." For the time being, the six counties of Ulster that make up Northern Ireland have escaped a Hobbesian state of nature, a development that is to be heartily welcomed. But it would be seriously wrong to call the present arrangements a victory for the rule of law, resulting in a normal democratic society.

ANARCHIST DELIRIUM

Burleigh dedicates a second historical chapter to "black" terrorism, the theory and practice of anarchism. The anarchists were practitioners of "propaganda by deed." Their unrelenting campaign of terror and assassinations in the late nineteenth and early twentieth centuries against kings, presidents, and the members of high society alike gave rise to an almost hysterical fear of a "universal conspiracy" to undermine the very foundations of civilized order. Some theorists of anarchism, such as the Russian Prince Kropotkin, eschewed "mindless terror" such as "chucking bombs into restaurants and theaters." At the same time, they incoherently welcomed the "multiplier effects" of violence that gave rise to "one evil deed" being "repaid with another," as Burleigh writes. This, they hoped, would lead to a "spiral of violence that would duly undermine the most repressive of governments." Their ire was directed against the "structural violence" of bourgeois societies and not the terrorist deeds of those who wished to establish a social order without hierarchy or coercion.

Other theoreticians of anarchism more openly advocated terror as an end in itself. The German Karl Heinzen wrote a bloodcurdling essay in 1852, "Murder," which called on his fellow revolutionaries to live and breathe murder as their overarching "motto," "answer," "need," "argument," and "refutation." As Burleigh points out, Heinzen believed that the revolutionaries of 1848 were too "weak-willed" to be effective or genuinely revolutionary. A new, bolder type of revolutionary needed, in Heinzen's words, to kill "all the representatives of the system of violence and murder which rules the world and lays it waste." For the anarchists, there had never been a truly *legitimate* political order in the whole of human history. Social order itself was a conspiracy by priests and princes against the rights and dignity of ordinary individuals. In a manner reminiscent of the Russian nihilists and the most fanatical of the Jacobin revolutionaries, Heinzen affirmed that "the road to humanity lies over the summit of cruelty." Like many other theorists of unlimited violence as an instrument of political and social emancipation, Heinzen combined moral and social perfectionism with a nihilistic indulgence of "indiscriminate terrorism." But this man of fierce and "fertile imagination" himself never hurt a fly. He even settled down into a life of charmed domesticity after he moved to the United States and took up residence in Boston in 1860.

Other anarchists were attracted to violence as a way of life because it was "unencumbered with theories that seemed to frustrate action." Burleigh concentrates on the case of Johann Most, the German anarchist-terrorist who was derided by his critics as "General Boom Boom" for his unremitting advocacy of "propaganda by deed." In Most's memorable and unnerving words, the task of the anarchist was to "shoot, burn, stab, poison, and bomb." Most, too, ended up in North America, where he became Emma Goldman's lover, a crowd-pleaser on the radical speakers' circuit, and a theoretician of terror by dynamite. Anarchists such as Most were actively involved in promoting—and attempting to radicalize—the massive labor unrest in the United States in the

1880s. The agitation was real enough but the reaction, Burleigh convincingly argues, was unfortunately often overwrought.

There was indeed a loose "Black International" committed to extirpating "bourgeois civilization." This was not, as some scholars insist, "a product of fevered bourgeois imaginations." But this loose, decentralized anarchist movement was taken by many in positions of authority as a "single conspiracy" both vast and mysterious. Many blamed it for "a welter of terrorist atrocities," just as al-Qaeda is sometimes blamed for, "and opportunistically takes credit for," terrorist acts that are the result of local or individual initiatives.

There is a salutary warning implicit in Burleigh's discussion of "black" terrorism. Anarchists in France, Spain, Italy, Britain, and the United States engaged in random attacks of violence, blowing up sundry cafes, government buildings, and opera houses, and even striking at Greenwich Park in London. Between 1894 and 1901, there was a spate of assassinations of heads of state (the prime minister of Spain, the King of Italy, and President William McKinley were among the victims) that made this period "more lethal for rulers than any other in modern history." However horrible these displays of anarchist violence were, they never came close to unseating legitimate state authority or uprooting the foundations of civilized order. But fearful of an encroaching, all-encompassing anarchist conspiracy, leaders and people sometimes lost their heads. The city of Chicago built a "huge fortified Armoury in the city" and insisted on basing a regular army division just thirty miles away to keep the anarchist hordes at bay. President Theodore Roosevelt fulminated against the anarchist pestilence and new immigration laws aimed to keep real or imagined anarchists out of the country. A vigilant response to anarchist terrorism was both prudent and necessary. But it was also necessary to keep such threats in perspective and not succumb to the apocalyptic illusion that "everything" is somehow different as a result of the violence unleashed by nihilistic murders (as was sometimes claimed after the 9/11 terrorist attacks on the United States).

That is the lesson that Burleigh draws from the writings of the great Anglo-Polish novelist Joseph Conrad. The anarchists described in his 1907 classic *The Secret Agent* were loosely modeled on such nihilist and anarchist terrorists as Mikhail Bakunin, Johann Most, and some of the principal Fenian dynamiters of the time. Conrad vividly describes petty, shabby men whose "moral squalor" stands out "beneath their grandiose apocalyptic talk." Their urge to destroy gives them an illusory sense of "power and personal prestige." This combination of personal shabbiness with a grandiose sense of self-importance and a nihilistic urge to destroy would characterize later incarnations of the terrorist impulse that Burleigh describes in his book. The Palestinian terrorists who made up the murderous "Black September" hit squads (who are most remembered for their unconscionable attack on the Israeli Olympic team in Munich in 1972), the "spoiled rich kids" who made up the Italian Red Brigades and the German Baader-Meinhof gang in the 1970s and 1980s, and the Saudi and Egyptian terrorists who plotted and carried out the deadly 9/11 terror attacks, are all richly illumined by a meditation on Conrad's portrait of the squalid personalities who are the perpetrators of modern terrorism. Burleigh recognizes that such a meditation is no substitute for a firm response to those who dedicate themselves "to the destruction of what is," as the lunatic Professor puts it in *The Secret Agent*. But such reflection provides inoculation against the temptation to romanticize or sympathize with or in any way exculpate terrorists whose "infernal doctrines" add "moral insanity" to "moral squalor."

The Nihilist Temptation

In chapter 2 of *Blood and Rage*, Burleigh returns to a theme that is also central to *Earthly Powers* and *Sacred Causes*, namely the conversion of a segment of the Russian intelligentsia to the cause of revolutionary nihilism. As Burleigh pointedly observes, belonging to the Russian intelligentsia had nothing to do per se with being educated or being a member of the professional classes. Rather, the intelligentsia was a subsection of the educated classes marked by "conformist subscription to such supposedly progressive ideas as atheism, socialism, and revolution." The Russian intelligentsia and even the Western-minded liberals who belonged to the Kadet or Constitutional Democratic Party refused to see enemies to the Left or condemn terrorism in principle. They indulged political forces in Russia who were adamantly opposed to reform, however beneficial to the lives of ordinary Russians. The "populist" terrorists of the 1860s and 1870s tried to undermine the Tsar Liberator Alexander II, who had abolished serfdom, modernized law courts and the army, introduced trial by jury, established self-governing *zemstva* or councils in rural Russia, and allowed an element of autonomy in Russian universities. When Tsar Alexander was assassinated by the terrorists of the "People's Will" in 1881, he was on the verge of introducing an advisory council, including elected representatives of civil society, that would have brought Russia closer to constitutional governance. His assassination only emboldened reactionaries and led to a quarter century of tight-fisted autocratic rule.

Dostoevsky was the most astute and profound critic of a nihilism that he predicted would lead to a form of oppression unprecedented in human experience. Burleigh cites and then comments on the eerily prophetic words that Dostoevsky puts into the mouth of the nihilist Shigalev in his masterpiece *The Possessed* (which is more accurately rendered as *Demons*):

> "I am perplexed by my own data and my conclusion is a direct contradiction of the idea from which I start. Starting from unlimited freedom, I arrive at absolute despotism. I will add, however, that there can be no solution of the social problem but mine." He foresees the death of "a hundred million" to realize a utopia that involves total spying designed to eliminate the private realm. In order to achieve human equality, "Cicero will have his tongue cut out, Copernicus will have his eyes put out, Shakespeare will be stoned."

Instead of judiciously attempting to meld the best Russian cultural and spiritual traditions with constitutionalism and the rule of law, polite society turned a blind eye to the "metaphysical madness" (to cite Burke's formulation again) proffered by Russia's revolutionary "demons." When the populist revolutionary Vera Zasulich (a sometime correspondent of Marx's) shot and wounded the police chief of St. Petersburg in broad daylight in January 1877, a jury of her peers had the temerity to acquit her. This indulgence toward left-wing terrorism would continue even after the introduction of a constitutional order (and elected parliament) in Russia in October 1905. The terrorist People's Will movement and its allies, for all their sound and fury, killed fewer than one hundred people, even if one of them was the tsar. The Social Revolutionary and Marxist radicals who terrorized Russia from 1906 onward killed thousands, including untold numbers of innocent civilians even as they engaged in open banditry.

They met their match in the figure of Pyotr Stolypin, prime minister of Russia from 1906–1911 and a statesman of unusual intelligence and determination. Stolypin was committed to crushing revolutionary terror once and for all, making Russia's peasants true citizen proprietors, and establishing a state that was both strong and free. Stolypin, the last best hope for Russia choosing the path of intelligent reform over nihilistic revolution, was gunned down by Dmitri Bogrov, a double agent of the secret police and the Social Revolutionaries, at the Kiev opera house in August 1911. When a Russian imperial state that was weakened by a protracted world war succumbed to revolutionary storms in February 1917, the path was open for the most self-assured, best-organized, and conspiratorial of Russia's revolutionary sects to come to power. The Bolsheviks, committed to state terrorism as a matter of policy (their goal was to "purge Russia of all the harmful insects"—"enemies of the people," as Lenin put it in a text that he wrote for himself in January 1918), freely drew upon the violent habits and talents of some of the demons of old.

Russia's liberals were not simply the "good guys" in a struggle between the autocratic Right and the revolutionary Left. In fact, Burleigh writes, "'liberalism' was represented by the revolutionary Kadets with their soft tolerance of appalling terrorist violence." These are the same soft liberals who ruled Russia for a few brief months after the February Revolution of 1917 and who prepared the way for the Bolsheviks to come to power during the October revolution of that year. This pattern of left-liberal indulgence of, or at least blindness to, totalitarianism and revolutionary terrorism would to a remarkable extent repeat itself in Western Europe in the 1960s and 1970s. Writing in 1972 in his Nobel lecture, Aleksandr Solzhenitsyn suggested that something like a Russian-style intelligentsia was in the process of being reborn among West European intellectual elites. These fashionable elites were enslaved to what Dostoevsky had earlier called "progressive little notions." Like their ideological forebears of one hundred years before, these left-liberal intellectuals refused to acknowledge enemies to the Left. In a fascinating chapter, "Guilty White Kids: The Red Brigades and the Red Army Faction," Burleigh provides a great deal of evidence to support this judgment. In the process, he vividly restores a moment in the history of European democracy that we forget at our peril.

"IDEOLOGY ADDICTION" OR THE
TURN TO TERRORISM IN WESTERN EUROPE

In discussing the intellectual climate in Western Europe during the 1960s and 1970s, Burleigh aptly refers to demi-intellectuals who had become "ideology addicts." For fifteen years, Italy was torn apart by leftist terrorists, principally the Red Brigades, but also by rival and derivative groups of "armed sectarian grouplets" such as the Prima Linea. Between 1969 and 1987, Italy saw 14,591 terrorist attacks, with 419 people being killed and another 1,182 people being wounded. Some militants on the extreme Right, disillusioned with the neofascist Italian Social Movement's efforts to enter the mainstream of Italian politics, and hoping to necessitate "the formation of an authoritarian state," unleashed several major bomb attacks that took the lives of 193 people. But the Red Brigades posed the major existential threat. They freely targeted representatives of the Italian state and judiciary, prominent businessman, and those in the academic and intellectual worlds who had the courage to criticize their nefarious deeds.

The era was marked by "conformist experimentation" and by what Burleigh aptly calls "visceral moralizing passion" occasioned by one-sided disdain for bourgeois society and by anger about "remote conflicts" in Latin America and Southeast Asia. The universities were, he writes, "one pool of a fanaticism that would fuel almost two decades of Red terrorism." In Italy, terrorists (and their intellectual apologists) were drawn from dissidents from both Roman Catholicism and the Italian Communist Party. Secular and religious progressives came together in support of the radical messianic transformation of the existing order. Throughout Western Europe, there was a tendency to see "fascism" everywhere. Italian and German intellectuals, in particular, lost the ability to distinguish between authoritarianism and authoritative institutions. The members of Italy's Red Brigades and West Germany's Red Army Faction, as well as their ideological sympathizers, could see no difference between liberal democracy, however imperfect and prosaic, and a militarized totalitarian state.

In Germany, radical lawyers manipulated the legal system to pass messages and provide material support to convicted terrorists. Some eventually became terrorists themselves. Left-liberal activists shamelessly compared the fate of pampered terrorist convicts to those of Jews in Auschwitz. In Italy, the fashionable radical ideologue Antonio Negri moved from left Catholicism to left-revolutionary terrorism with hardly a thought. Soon he was involved in terrorist activities himself, fleeing to France just as his parliamentary immunity was about to be removed. After returning to Italy many years later and spending six years in jail, Negri would travel the globe as a celebrity intellectual. *Empire* (2000), an unreadable critique of capitalist globalization that he cowrote with Duke professor Michael Hardt, remains an important intellectual point of reference in the leftist enclave of the academy known as "cultural studies." For his part, Jean-Paul Sartre, that indefatigable defender of revolutionary tyranny and terror, would visit the German terrorist Andreas Baader in his prison cell to give support to Baader's unfounded complaints about the "atrocious" conditions under which he was held. Privately, Sartre admitted to being repelled by Baader and muttered to friends that he was an "arsehole." So much for the good faith of the self-proclaimed "philosopher of freedom."

Most West European intellectuals did not go nearly as far as Negri or Sartre in their support for revolutionary nihilism. But this period in West European history saw an explosion in radical sentimentality and grotesque self-hatred among some of the principal beneficiaries of liberal civilization. In this it resembles the intellectual and cultural climate that came to predominate in Russia from the 1860s onward. As Burleigh points out, by the late 1960s the radical Left no longer had faith in the liberating propensities of Soviet socialism. That regime had become too bureaucratic and sclerotic to be a plausible object of utopian hopes. As we have already discussed in chapter five, they instead looked to faraway regimes and leaders about whom they knew little or nothing—Castro and Guevara in Cuba, Mao and Chou En-lai in China. More typically, they supported revolution as the negation of what they saw as the ultimate evil—the "repressive tolerance" of bourgeois society—and imagined that a free and humane future would somehow arise out of such a revolutionary negation. This surely qualifies as "moral insanity."

Thankfully, public opinion remained broadly conservative, consistently supporting parties and governments of the center-right and center-left against extremists. In time, Western governments drew on the crucial testimony of repentant terrorists, the exhaustion and self-destruction of armed messianic movements, and increasingly effective counterterrorism measures to put an end to this twenty-year eruption of ideological madness. The question remains why an influential segment of the European elite showed sympathy for armed revolutionaries who were addicted to ideological abstractions and oblivious to the real political options available within modern democratic industrial societies. Burleigh rightly argues that in contrast to the terrorist movements of the 1960s and 1970s, it is impossible for progressive intellectuals to sympathize with the ideological goals of radical Islamists. What *soi-disant* radical hopes for a universal Islamic caliphate and the establishment of a draconian version of Sharia law? But a residue of the old revolutionary nihilism persists in progressive intellectual circles today. The West is still seen as an essentially "culpable" civilization. Many intellectuals and demi-intellectuals are willing to excuse or at least relativize the crimes of the West's most fanatical enemies. Meanwhile, European elites tend to take for granted that law-enforcement measures that were finally adequate for dealing with homegrown domestic terrorism in Italy or Germany, or that were the principal means for fighting ETA or the IRA, will be sufficient for dealing with the global threat posed by al-Qaeda and other Islamic extremists. There is, alas, little evidence to support this excessively sunny judgment.

ISLAM AND ISLAMISM: RELIGION AND POLITICAL RELIGION

In the longest chapter of his book ("World Rage: Islamist Terrorism"), Burleigh returns to the analysis of Islam he had already pursued in the tenth and final chapter of *Sacred Causes* ("Cubes, Domes and Death Cults: Europe after 9/11"). In both chapters, Burleigh recounts the events leading up to the terror attacks of September 11, 2001. He provides a thorough account of the intellectual roots of Islamic extremism from Sayyid Qutb, the anti-Western ideologist whose writings inspired the Muslim Brotherhood, to the deranged "Occidentalism" (the West as the root of all evil), anti-Semitism, and conscienceless promotion of global terror by Osama bin Laden and his al-Qaeda network. But in *Sacred Causes* Burleigh unfortunately overstated the case when he suggested that Islamist terrorism was in important respects "a cover version of ideas and movements that have occurred in modern western societies." As a result, he conceded too much to terms like "Islamofascism" and "Islamo-Bolshevism" that in retrospect confuse more than they clarify.

Burleigh had been careful throughout *Sacred Causes* to avoid the "terrible simplification," so widespread in our time, that transforms an ideological movement of some historical specificity—fascism—into a broad symbol of everything repressive, authoritarian, and violence-prone. Fascism had a particularly ferocious bark (Mussolini ostentatiously proclaimed its totalitarian aspirations) but the least impressive bite of any of the political religions of the twentieth century. To be sure, Islamist currents owe something to the Western totalitarian aversion to the deracination characteristic of mass urban industrial society. But it is a mistake to see them as a mere "cover version," a local religious variant, of twentieth-century European totalitarianism.

In *Blood and Rage*, Burleigh engages in an important self-correction. He is now more skeptical of terms such as "Islamofascist" and "Islamo-Bolshevik," both because of their imprecision and because they risk "indicting" Islam as a whole. They also risk confusing all forms of Islamic fundamentalism with terrorist extremism. Burleigh now speaks of salafist-jihadists who declare "holy war" on infidels and those they see as pseudo-Muslims. Those who yearn for the restoration of Islamic glory support the establishment of a universal Islamic caliphate and "seek to bring about the violent transformation of [Islamic] societies into Islamic states." The salafist clerics and theoreticians dream of a utopia where Muslims rededicate themselves to "the wise founders who surrounded Mohammed." This dream entails historical revisionism of the worst sort since Islam has been endemically prone to division—an "empire without an emperor" in the words of one scholar—since the death of Mohammed.

Burleigh is right to distinguish salafist-jihadist Islam from Islam *tout court*. But the "willfulness" of the radicals, rejecting the restraints of the moral law and the dignity inherent in man as man, draws upon powerful currents within historic Islam itself. This is a dilemma which confronts everyone dedicated to a moderate course for Muslims in the modern world. The radical voluntarism of a God whose Will refuses to bow even to his Reason and Goodness, the division of humanity into the "house of submission" and "the house of war," a tradition of reducing the other "peoples of the book" to *dhimmitude* or worse, the absence of any fundamental distinction between the things of God and the things of Caesar—all of these are ingredients of Islamic radicalism that have some roots in historic Islam itself (these themes are addressed with great insight and precision in Pope Benedict XVI's widely misunderstood September 2006 Regensburg address). The emphasis of the radicals is one-sided and ignores any mitigating tendencies within the broader Islamic tradition. But the key point should not be evaded: the Islamists creatively added some distinctively modern ideological ingredients—as well as a strictly utilitarian attitude to modern technology—to an already volatile mix.

CONCLUSION

In the final pages of his book Burleigh calls for Western governments to engage in a sustained effort at public diplomacy and cultural outreach to the hundreds of millions of Muslims in the Middle East who "do not savor dictation by mullahs." He is particularly critical of the multicultural delusions and soft political correctness that for many years impeded efforts to deal with the threat of radical Islam in countries like Britain and the Netherlands. He yearns for a time when tough-minded "theologians like Reinhold Niebuhr and Paul Tillich knew how to respond to evil without limp equivocation." A self-proclaimed "conservative realist," Burleigh rejects both the excesses of neoconservatism and the European tendency to reduce the struggle against terrorism to a matter of effective policing and law enforcement. His practical suggestions are for the most part sober and sensible and are likely to provoke only those who deny that the Western world is engaged in a "war on terror," however problematic that expression remains. Yet the real interest of his book lies elsewhere. *Blood and Rage* stands apart from other works on the subject because it is that rare book that expands our historical memory and has the power to shape mature moral and political judgment. In addition to shedding light on the distressing indulgence of many modern intellectuals toward tyranny and terrorism in their various forms, Burleigh's work provides much needed guidance for confronting the threat posed by Islamism to civilized values. At the same time, it provides a salutary warning against exaggerating the existential threat such a movement poses to Western civilization. Such prudent but tough-minded conservative realism is particularly needed in our time.

Part V

A Model of Moderate and Humane Conservatism

9

Raymond Aron's Model of
Democratic Conservatism

We have already had several occasions to discuss the political reflection of Raymond Aron (1905–1983), a conservative-minded liberal who provides the imitable model of the political philosopher as civic educator. It is fitting to end our consideration of the conservative foundations of the liberal order with an examination of Aron's rich, measured, and dialectical conception of "democratic conservatism." His life and writings embodied the best legacy of the Enlightenment while showing that the defense of liberty demanded courage and moderation as well as thoughtful, self-critical, yet unhesitating fidelity to the inheritance that is Western civilization.

In his columns in *Le Figaro* (1947–1977) and *L'Express* (1977–1983) and in articles in journals such as *Liberté de l'Esprit, Preuves, Encounter, Contrepoint,* and *Commentaire,* Aron commented brilliantly on the great issues of the day. But he was careful to distinguish his political commentary from his "scientific" works. He never lost sight of the distinction between the philosopher and other intellectual types: the intellectual prone to partisanship, the sophist, and the ideologue. His cherished intellectual ideal was "equity," a truly balanced approach to historical and political understanding. Of course, he had a political perspective and took political stands in the great controversies of his time.

Aron was a conservative-minded liberal who belonged to the "party of the Center" in France—the party of Constant, Tocqueville, and Élie Halévy—that sought a middle path between revolutionary romanticism and reactionary nostalgia. As such, he was an eloquent critic of what Tocqueville called "literary politics," the tendency of modern intellectuals to judge prosaic but decent democratic societies by utopian standards that had never been—and could never be—actualized. He had no sympathy for Third World radicalism but as early as 1956 he argued for the inevitability of Algerian independence on largely practical or pragmatic grounds. A critic of the centralized French university that he thought was badly in need of reform, he was, as we have seen, the most vocal critic of the assault on the liberal university in May 1968. As Pierre Manent has observed, while no apologist for Gaullism, Aron was appalled by the thought that the French Fifth Republic could be brought down by the revolutionary agitations of Daniel Cohn-Bendit and his ilk.

In my view, Aron is best understood, at least in his public role, as a civic educator. He addressed political questions from the point of view of the responsible citizen and statesman and when offering political advice to his fellow citizens always asked, "What would I do if I were in the place of the ministers?" There was a largeness to his views that was admired by people along the ideological spectrum (although some on the intellectual Left persisted for far too long in the perverse belief that "it was better to be wrong with Sartre than right with Aron"). In France today, there is a growing tendency for men of the Left to soften Aron, to claim him for social democracy, for the camp of left-liberalism. The great stumbling block to this appropriation is Aron's anti-Communism, his consistent support for the parties of the center-right in the years after World War II, and his contempt for "the thought of '68," the hodgepodge of anarchism, postmodernism, left-libertarianism, and antinomianism that he believed to be *one* decisive influence on the so-called May events.

Aron's public engagement over a fifty-year period was guided by a distinctive notion of democratic conservatism central to his understanding of political responsibility. In the age of ideology, Aron challenged the complacency of democratic elites and acted as a civic educator in a French society riven by ideological divisions that were far more pronounced than those present in the more stable democracies of the Anglo-Saxon world. But there is much that the citizens of the English-speaking democracies can learn from Raymond Aron's efforts at overcoming ideological modes of thought and action, from his practice of political responsibility, and from his model of moderate and humane conservatism.

Breaking Free from "Facile Progressivism"

Aron had begun the 1930s as a pacifist and socialist; his political convictions were more or less indistinguishable from the majority of his peers in a left-liberal secular Parisian milieu. The turning point for Aron—the truly formative stage in his political education—was the three years he spent in a Germany on the edge of the abyss. As a reader at the University of Cologne and then as a resident of the Maison Académique in Berlin, Aron witnessed the death throes of the Weimar Republic and the rise of a monstrously self-confident National Socialist movement. As Aron pointed out in his 1970 inaugural address ("On the Historical Condition of the Sociologist") at the Collège de France, it was during these years that he cured himself of "facile progressivism"—the belief that "history automatically obeys the dictates of reason"—and "held on, not without effort to hope." His direct experience of the rise of National Socialism in Germany—the burning of suspect books in Berlin made a particular impression on him—led him to reject in important respects the education he had received at the French university.

The spirit that animated that education was, in Aron's view, lacking in a sense of the tragic, oblivious to the political realities that might be discerned from an attentive reading of Aristotle and Machiavelli, and too confident in the power of "positive" science to provide the "rational" foundations of a humanized world. The French university's dual confidence in science and socialism, its social determinism and "ineradicable optimism regarding long range outcomes," reached its apex in an apolitical "science of society" of the Durkheimian type. Such an approach—more *sociologism* than social science—had little to say about a world confronting unprecedented "historical storms" and Aron never ceased to express his "allergy" toward it.

It was during his German sojourn that Aron discovered the thought of Max Weber and other representatives of German sociology. As Pierre Manent has put it, Weber—with his admirable intellectual probity and love of truth, his defense of historical indeterminacy, his pessimism regarding the ultimate reconciliation of science and human values—was the "hero" of Aron's youth. The mature Aron would later come to have and express grave doubts regarding the excessive pathos and "Nietzschean nihilism" that he came to see beneath the surface of Weber's austere methodological reflections. Aron continued to believe that the "limits of science, the antinomies of thought and action" as articulated by Weber, are "authentic contributions to a phenomenological description of the human condition." But he rejected Weber's translation of these into a "philosophy of discord" that denied reason's capacity *qua* reason "to differentiate between vitalistic values and reasonable accomplishment; its hypotheses include the total irrationality of choices between political parties or among the various images of the world in conflict, and the moral and spiritual equivalence of various attitudes—those of the sage and the madman, of the fanatic and of the moderate."

This is not the occasion to discuss Aron's debt to and divergences from Weber's sociological and philosophical reflection.[1] The debt is great as are the accompanying differences and divergences. Suffice it to say that in articulating his own response to the tragedies of the twentieth century, Aron moved beyond German sociology to draw upon the more capacious intellectual and spiritual resources of the broader Western political and philosophical traditions. His "Weberianism," his most precious intellectual acquisition of the 1930s, was subsequently moderated and supplemented by a turn to a wide array of thinkers—Aristotle, Tocqueville, and Montesquieu among them—who provided a firmer ground than Weber could for Aron's choice for decency and moderation over fanaticism in all its forms.

Aron's Voice: The June 17, 1939, Address

Aron's "conservative liberalism," or "democratic conservatism," as he sometimes called it, was evident early on in the address on "Democratic States and Totalitarian States" that he delivered to the French Philosophical Society on June 17, 1939. This address and the arguments that inform it are essential for understanding the political philosophy that guided Raymond Aron's interventions in French (and Western) political and intellectual debates over the course of the next forty-five years. It is the view of political responsibility informing that presentation that separates Aron from the posturing literary politics—a mixture of naïveté, leftist dogmatism, and self-dramatizing "commitment"—that was typical of all too many intellectuals in his time—and ours.

"Democratic States and Totalitarian States" is remarkable not least because of the authoritative tone that informs it from beginning to end. Aron's "voice" is inseparable from his argument. Speaking to an audience that included some of the most influential prewar French intellectuals, the thirty-four-year-old Aron presents his argument with an authority, a reasoned self-confidence that belied his relatively marginal status in French intellectual life at that time. He was a man without an academic position; only a year earlier, he had defended his controversial doctoral thesis, *Introduction à la philosophie de l'Histoire*. That work forcefully challenged the intellectual foundations of positivism and historical progressivism even as it elicited fevered charges that Aron had succumbed to pessimism and despair and to a thoroughgoing historical relativism. To be sure, Aron's gifts were widely recognized and he was close to distinguished sociologists and philosophers such as C. Bouglé and Élie Halévy, who were at the center, or close to the center, of French intellectual life. Yet one cannot overstate the radical character of the challenge that Aron posed to a French intellectual class that was content with its progressivist illusions and seemingly oblivious to the coming war that was about to shatter what was left of liberal Europe.

Aron attempts to alert his interlocutors to the dangers posed by the imperialism of the new "revolutionary" states, particularly National Socialist Germany, and by the decadence and lack of collective resolve of the established European democracies, especially France. He was convinced that while war was just around the corner, the democracies were oblivious to the real nature of the enemy and to the urgent steps that must be taken to renew the democratic states. Aron's choice of the word "revolutionary" to characterize National Socialist Germany could not but antagonize those in his audience who were committed to an antifascist ideology that identified revolution with the sacrosanct principles of 1789, showed indulgence toward the totalitarians of the Left, and that mistook the new German and Italian elites for a militarized form of aristocratic and capitalist domination.

Aron disdained this "ideological" distortion of reality. While the new totalitarian elites had successfully co-opted older Italian and German elites and used them for their own purposes, they were fundamentally revolutionary in character, imbued with a deep hatred of both Christian ethics and a "bourgeois" ethos which they mistook for a "corrupt" preference for hedonism and utilitarianism over the highest human ideals. The new revolutionary elites not only rejected "the old forms of family life, of university and intellectual life," but repudiated those virtues—"respect for the person, respect for the mind, for personal autonomy"—that were at the heart of liberal civilization. The "virtues" the totalitarians cultivated in their place were "essentially virtues of a military character, virtues of action, of ascetism, of devotion."

RENEWING DEMOCRACY ON CONSERVATIVE FOUNDATIONS

Against a complacent antifascist ideology, preoccupied as it was with a mythological distinction between the good Left and bad Right, Aron reminded his listeners that in the new international context the democracies were essentially "conservative," defenders of the acquisitions of Christian and liberal civilization against the militarism-*cum*-nihilism of the totalitarians. In response to the totalitarian threat, he calls for a renewal of liberalism on the foundation of a broad-based "democratic conservatism." No less than any other viable, self-respecting human order, liberal communities needed to draw upon the devotion and virtue of their citizens. It was childish or worse to evoke "fascism" every time someone proposed bolstering the authority of the state or following certain methods that were also used by "the regimes we are combating."

Aron's newly articulated conservatism was firmly liberal in character. He freely recognized that there were "limits to the interventions and coercion of the State" and that there "exist social and economic conditions which are peculiar to a government of liberty." At a time when classical liberalism was thoroughly discredited among European intellectuals, Aron insisted that there could be no political liberty without a "certain freedom of the economy." While liberal societies were thus obliged to reject the militarization of the state and the economy, they must aim to rebuild a "ruling elite"—the words are Aron's—"which is neither cynical, nor cowardly, which has political courage without falling into pure and simple Machiavellianism." This ruling elite must have confidence in itself and must work to "restore in the democratic governments a minimum of faith or of common will."

Aron proceeds to articulate a conception of democratic authority in which elites have learned to distinguish what is "essential" to the democratic idea from what is false and self-destructive in it. In accord with the best conservative-liberal traditions, he insists that the "sovereignty of the people" is not an essential idea since it "can lead to despotism as easily as to liberty." What *is* essential is legality or the rule of law and a decent respect for human beings as *persons* and not merely as instruments for the "means of production or as objects of propaganda." This notion of the human being as a person imbued with conscience and dignity is indebted to the Kantian, liberal, and biblical traditions and is an essential element of Aron's political and philosophical reconciliation of liberalism and conservatism.

The reinvigorated conception of democratic authority that Aron has in mind is neither "magical nor irrational." It is not automatically validated by some abstract ideology of "popular sovereignty." Aron fears that without faith in themselves and without a "minimum of competence" in administering complex modern societies, decadent democracies would all too readily give way to "that peculiar mixture of demagogy, technique, irrational faith and police force" that reigned in totalitarian states such as National Socialist Germany.

At the end of his address, Aron speaks openly and unapologetically about the "form of conservatism that I would like to defend." This conservatism requires "elementary virtues of discipline, consent to authority and technical competence" that had been co-opted by the totalitarian enemies of civilization. It also demands intellectual courage, "the courage to question everything and make clear the problems on which the very existence of a country like France depends."

Aron's Response to His Critics

Aron's June 17, 1939, address was met by anger and consternation as well as by rarer expressions of agreement and admiration. Even those who were in general agreement with his analysis, such as the Thomistic philosopher and Christian Democratic theorist Jacques Maritain, were surprised and somewhat taken back by his characterization of modern democracies as "conservative" societies. In his response to Aron, Maritain agreed that it was necessary to cultivate the "heroic virtues" in democracies. But he worried that if the democracies borrowed totalitarian techniques and virtues they would gradually become like the very regimes they set out to resist.

Aron's response to Maritain's concerns was friendly, forceful, and revealing. In principle he agreed that the virtues he invoked, including heroism, had been co-opted by a radically different understanding of the common good and the political order than the one he preferred. The heroic virtues were manipulated and distorted by totalitarian propaganda machines that sought to reduce human beings to the status of soldiers in militarized despotisms. Still, Aron had no time for the "really stupid thought," dear to many on the pacifist Left, that "as soon as one attempts to resist, one compromises the reasons for resisting." Such arguments had been used to oppose conscription in England and other efforts to prepare the democracies for the inevitable coming of war. Every people who wish to endure, Aron insisted, "must have a minimum of will to power, of consent to violence." One of the illusions of democratic humanitarianism was to simply identify that will with totalitarianism rather than recognizing it as an essential element of the political instinct.

Aron reiterated in the discussion that followed his talk that he refused to lend a "value factor" to the term revolutionary and a "negative factor to the term conservative." The democracies *were* fundamentally conservative "in the sense that they wish to conserve the traditional values upon which our civilization is founded" against those who wish to establish a wholly militarized society. Those who wish to preserve free societies are necessarily both conservative and liberal: like Aron, they reject "the radical destruction of our present society" even as they fight "to save for individuals something of personal dignity and autonomy."

In response to the vituperations of the antifascist thinker Victor Basch, Aron denounced the political infantilism of a French antifascist movement that needlessly polarized French public opinion (making a united antitotalitarian front by the moderate Left and Right all the more difficult) and that showed limitless indulgence toward the totalitarian Left. He also lambasted the economic demagogy of France's Popular Front government and its addiction to "idiotic measures" which served to diminish the workday by 20 percent—even as they increased salaries by 50 percent. Aron had already limned such a critique—in a more measured tone—in an article in the *Revue de métaphysique et de morale* in 1936. But his denunciation of the "abstract moralism" of the contemporary partisans of the ideas of 1789—although not of the ideas themselves—marked his first systematic assault on what he would later call in *The Opium of the Intellectuals* "the myth of the Left." A certain "abstract moralism and progressivism" served to obscure the concrete ways in which "respect for the person and for the mind" could be preserved in the context of twentieth-century politics. Aron's conservative case for democracy, articulated with lucidity and directness in the June 17, 1939, address, aimed self-consciously to limn a principled third way between Machiavellian cynicism and humanitarian moralism.

The most impressive contribution to the discussion came from Étienne Mantoux, an accomplished student and protégé of the conservative liberal historian and philosopher Élie Halévy, and the author of the definitive response to Keynes's book on *The Economic Consequences of the Peace.* The twenty-six-year-old Mantoux, a conservative-minded liberal devoid of humanitarian sentimentality, warmly praised Aron for showing "that one can admire democracy without failing to recognize its faults, that one can love liberty without becoming sentimental, and that 'he who loves well punishes well.'" Mantoux went on to distinguish true liberals, who have an essential role to play in conserving the values of Western civilization, from the false liberals who have "their tails between their legs" and are unwilling to *defend* either political and economic liberty. Mantoux's authoritative—almost Ciceronian—intervention provides a description *avant la lettre* of the virtues that would inform Aron's political and intellectual engagement for the next half century.

Aron's address on "Democratic States and Totalitarian States" and the discussion that followed are memorable not least because of the juxtaposition between his lucidity regarding the totalitarian threat, the imminence of war, and the steps that were necessary to renew the "decadent" democracies, and the complacent progressivism and moralism of so many of his interlocutors. Amply evident in this address is the democratic conservatism

171

that was henceforth coextensive with Aronian liberalism. That democratic conservatism or conservative liberalism was given particularly moving expression in the essays that Aron wrote for the Free French journal of culture and ideas *La France Libre* during World War II. Aron played an essential role as editor of a journal that was sponsored by de Gaulle and the Gaullists without ever being a mere propaganda vehicle for that movement. The essays that Aron wrote for *La France Libre* are the closest things he ever penned to a political and spiritual credo, to a work of public philosophy outlining the moral foundations of a renewed liberalism that would have learned decisive political and spiritual lessons from the experience of totalitarianism.

"REAFFIRMING THE SPIRITUAL MISSION OF HUMANITY"

Aron, a self-described atheist or agnostic, nonetheless recoiled from the various philosophical and political manifestations of modern nihilism. In a series of lucid essays informed by no small dose of pathos, Aron repudiated the entire line of modern thought from Machiavelli to Nietzsche that exalted the human will as the foundation and end or purpose of collective life. He provided a genealogy of modern extremism—of the nihilism and historical pessimism informing fascist and protofascist thought—and deepened his search for a third way between cynicism and facile progressivism. In a powerful 1942 essay "Tyrannie et mépris des hommes" ("Tyranny and the Contempt for Man") that first appeared in the February 1942 issue of *La France Libre* and that was republished in Aron's 1946 collection *L'homme contre les tyrans*, Aron provided an expert dissection of the thought of the "pessimistic" Right going from Machiavelli to Nietzsche, Oswald Spengler, and Carl Schmitt. Of course National Socialism could not be blamed on any of these subtle and serious thinkers. But their "contempt for men" had provided powerful theoretical support to the "corruption dirigée"—the institutionalized and "directed" corruption which defined National Socialist despotism. Aron's 1942 essay reads like a *cri de coeur* decrying the scientism and crude "social biologism" that allowed the National Socialists to destroy human beings with impunity.

For Aron, it was not enough to militarily vanquish the Hitlerian evil, to defeat the National Socialist regime at war. The only way to definitively surmount nihilism—the hatred or contempt for man—was to "reaffirm the spiritual mission of humanity" with the full powers and cooperation of man's faith and reason. This had nothing to do with a historical optimism that was as estranged from the truth about men as the pessimism it tried to overcome through a counter act of the will. The events of the first half of the twentieth century had confirmed what thinking men already knew: man was a being open to the good but with certain pronounced tendencies to brutality and evil. Against both extremes, Aron declared his belief—a rational belief—in the human soul, a "presence which provided a foundation for dignity and the right to respect." In the essays collected in *L'homme contre les tyrans*, Aron repeatedly expresses his belief in the reality and ineffable dignity of the human soul. He spoke not as a believer—although he had great respect for the transcendental religions as opposed to the "secular" ones of the twentieth century—but as a philosopher, a human being, and a citizen. Modern totalitarianism had confirmed—negatively, so to speak—what Western philosophy and theology had always affirmed: man is unrecognizable other than as a being with conscience and moral responsibility. Man "must utilize his conscience in order to better accomplish his task of civilization and not to treat himself as a beast or to reduce himself to the level of an animal species." A renewed commitment to conscience—not as an abstract imperative, much less a myth or metaphor, but as an existential confirmation of man's spiritual nature and vocation—was a precondition for overcoming technobureaucratic despotism and the "era of contempt." Aron appreciated that the premodern religious and philosophical traditions of the West and important currents of modern philosophy could find common ground in a defense and convincing articulation of human dignity in response to the totalitarian assault on man.

The next crucial step had to be the renewal of a "faith without illusions" that drew lessons from the totalitarian episode even as it tried to renew liberal rationalism on deeper spiritual foundations. Aron's famous dissection of the Communist and National Socialist "secular religions"—"The Future of the Secular Religions," published in *La France Libre* in two parts in July and August 1944—ends with an invocation of the "revolt of conscience." It is conscience, informed by a respect for the truth that refuses to accept the ludicrous claims of totalitarian despots of both the Left and Right that their words somehow "define good and evil." But Aron goes on to insist that "nothing great in history is ever achieved unless the masses have faith in ideas and in men." Only with such faith will men sacrifice willingly for the cause of liberty and civilization. The precondition of such self-transcendence is an authentic confidence in the "spiritual mission of humanity."

Aron's Non Possum to Communism

After the Second World War, Aron increasingly turned his attention to the threat posed by Soviet Communism to Western liberty and human dignity. He was France's most intelligent and persevering critic of Communist totalitarianism, as well as the indulgence shown toward it by a full array of fellow-traveling intellectuals and philosophers (Merleau-Ponty and Sartre not least among them). In his newspapers columns in the Parisian daily *Le Figaro*, in impressive hybrid works such as *Le grande schisme* (1948) and *Les guerres en chaîne* (1951) that richly combined historical, political, and philosophical analysis, and in the essays collected in *Polémiques* (1955), Aron took aim at the "seduction of totalitarianism" and dissected the "superstition of History." Drawing on his own prewar writings on "the philosophy of history" Aron provided an account of the twentieth century that exploded the myths of "historical inevitability" and that did justice retrospectively to the roles of necessity, accident, and free human action in the unfolding of the great twentieth-century drama. As he eloquently put it in his classic 1955 work *The Opium of the Intellectuals*: "There is no such thing as global determinism. The transcendence of the future, for man in Time, is an incentive to will his own destiny and a guarantee that, whatever happens, hope will not perish."[2]

It perplexed and angered Aron that *soi-disant* defenders of "human emancipation," of social justice and solidarity, identified the human vocation with an ideological "pyramid builder" such as Stalin, who, along with Lenin, had built the other great camp society of the twentieth century. Perhaps even more than its cruelty and violence, Aron was appalled by the "enforced lie" that defined Communist theory and practice. Near the end of *Paix et guerre entre les nations* (which first appeared in French in 1962) he wrote that "because they have done something different from what they believed they would do, because they pursued inaccessible goals, goals contrary to the nature of men and societies, the Communists lie as perhaps no other great historical movement before them has ever lied." One hears the great theme of Solzhenitsyn's Nobel lecture, his *Letter to the Soviet Leaders*, and *The Gulag Archipelago* voiced a full decade or so before the publication of these definitive guides to the "ideological lie." It is not surprising, then, that Aron responded with respect and admiration for Solzhenitsyn's efforts to expose the evil of ideology: "The illusion that men and social organizations can be transformed at a stroke," as Aron strikingly put it in a 1976 essay on "Solzhenitsyn and Sartre."

Aron, the philosopher of history, was acutely aware of the temptation of retrospective fatalism, especially in a democratic age addicted to historicist assumptions. He knew that once events occurred it was tempting for our contemporaries to assume that these events were somehow inevitable all along. This temptation was present both during the Cold War and afterwards. Those thinkers and intellectuals who resisted the totalitarian temptation and worked to shape an intelligent anti-Communist consensus in the West would later be criticized for wasting their time fighting a movement that was in any case destined to collapse. In *Peace and War* Aron not only anticipates such historicist interpretations of the West's victory in the Cold War but provides a compelling response to this fundamentally corrupt line of thinking. He eloquently rebukes those who justify cowardice and abstention by historical detachment:

> That the totalitarian faith or purpose will eventually wither away it would be ungracious to deny, especially if one feels that totalitarianism is contrary to the eternal springs of human nature. But one would not be justified in deducing from this that the dogmatism of immanence, the claim to create a total man and a new man are merely superstructures or myths. Soviet society is indissolubly a group of institutions *and* the metaphysical intention of those who build it. That certain of these institutions may survive although emptied of the intention that inspires and distorts them is possible. But one cannot today consider this dissociation as already achieved. Our duty is to combat what we condemn and not to assume in advance the privileges of the pure spectator, as if our immedi-

ate future were already our distant past. I am the one who is deliberating and not my grandchildren. If they do not take the totalitarian threat as a tragedy, perhaps I may have helped to make their detachment possible by the very fact that I will have averted the danger. But to invoke a future detachment is really to seek an excuse for cowardice or abstention.

"Antinomic Prudence": The Role of Conservatism in Modern Societies

Some on the Left criticized Aron for not writing a critique of the "myth of the Right" comparable to the critique of the myths of the "Left," the "Proletariat," and "Revolution" he provided in the opening chapters of *The Opium of the Intellectuals*. Aron responded to this criticism with a remarkable 110-page essay entitled "De la droite: Le conservatisme dans les sociétés industrielles" ("On the Right: Conservatism in Industrial Societies") that appeared as the first part of his 1957 book *Espoir et peur du siècle (Hope and Fear of the Century)*. This essay and book, one of Aron's few pieces from that period that did not appear in English, are indispensable for appreciating the distinctive character of Aron's conservative liberalism, of the democratic conservatism that he had first articulated in the June 17, 1939, address to the French Philosophical Society. While extremely critical of currents on the French Right—whether the half-modernist salon monarchism of *Action française*, or a traditionalist Right that was nostalgic for a France that no longer existed, not to mention the fascist or semifascist currents associated with Vichy's "National Revolution"—Aron presented nothing like a total critique of the Right, or even a critique of "the myth of the Right" that was comparable to the critique of "the myth of the Left" that he had sketched in *The Opium of the Intellectuals*.

There is a reason for this asymmetry that has nothing to do with a double standard. As Aron makes clear in the final pages of his 1957 essay, a conservatism that is cognizant of contemporary problems and which "resolutely accepts the exigencies of industrial civilization would be authentically rational." Such a conservatism would not reproach ideologists for being "theoretical," in the manner of a certain kind of traditionalism, but rather for having "unilateral" or "erroneous" theories. Aron categorically states that the ideologies of the Left at that time, of which Communism was the "extreme expression," "deform the real." Aron does not include in this critique social democracy or various reformist programs for the renewal of Western societies. His target is the abstract moralism and progressivism that he had earlier taken aim at in June 1939. This moralism, when buttressed by a *Marxisant* "idolatry of History," becomes an excuse for a unilateral preference for some values—such as equality— over others—such as liberty and the "tradition of liberty"—that are equally vital for the functioning of a modern society of a liberal type. Democratic conservatism of the Aronian type does not "refuse analysis or abstraction." Nor does it denounce liberal principles, the principles of liberty and equality. Rather, it aims "to hold synoptically the multiple values that we are trying to safeguard."

Brian C. Anderson has aptly called this task of preserving indispensable but sometimes contradictory values "antinomic prudence." Such prudence aims to moderate democratic impatience and dispel the illusion that some values can be maximized without damaging other goods that are indispensable for a free and decent human life. When Aron harshly attacked the political and economic program of the "Union of the Left," the coalition of Communists and Socialist parties under the leadership of François Mitterrand, in a famous 1973 article in *Le Figaro* ("The Common Program of the Left: Or the Circle Squared"), he did so not as a doctrinaire of the market but in the name of liberty and a prudent sense of social reality. It was absurd to try to combine a redistribution of revenues in favor of the unfortunate, an ambitious program of industrial nationalizations, and state control of the entirety of the credit and banking sectors with the maintenance, even the acceleration, of growth.

Aron had no doubt that Mitterrand, unlike the quasi-Stalinist French Communist leader Georges Marchais, was at least in part inspired by "good intentions." But by ignorance and dogmatism, French socialists risked destroying the French economy and putting essential liberties at risk. When faced with a choice between maintaining a liberal polity and economy and radicalizing *la rupture* with capitalism in order to stem capital flight, President Mitterrand chose the path of prudence in March 1983, effectively putting an end to any efforts to implement a later version of the "Common Program of the Left." But as Aron pointed out at that time, Mitterrand never adequately explained his choice to the French people, thus allowing the socialist prejudice against the market economy to outlive the failure of socialist efforts to create another "logic" of society. Aron did not move to the Right in 1973 (or 1981) by opposing the Left's "deformation of the real" but rather remained faithful to the antinomic prudence he had first articulated in a somewhat less polarized period of French history.

In his 1957 essay on "Conservatism in Industrial Societies," Aron argues that the task for an intelligent conservatism in the modern world was to learn to distinguish the "eternal content" of conservative wisdom—the necessary defense of hierarchy, tradition, authority—from its "transitory content." The Right needed to make its peace with a contemporary civilization that was, for better or worse, "popular, industrial, materialist." The danger was not that conservative thought would degenerate into ideology and fanaticism in the manner of so much leftist thought in the twentieth century, but that it would give way to a "retrospective and sterile myth" about the good society that existed only in the imaginations of its adherents. A viable conservatism must recognize the legitimacy of egalitarian aspirations not only as a matter of justice but in order to moderate democratic impatience and to safeguard the full range of values that are integral to any social order.

It was imperative for the European Right to come to terms with the fact that under conditions of modernity the "progress of productivity" is essential to civic peace and national power, as well as to the satisfaction of basic human needs. An earlier conservative statesman like John Adams "doubted that any society would ever have the resources and solicitude to instruct all its children." Aron states emphatically that Adams was wrong. The egalitarian and Promethean ambitions of modern society no doubt risk raising unreasonable hopes about the ability of modern societies to maximize all the advantages of productivity, liberty, and equality. But the "movement of events . . . is oriented towards the Left" at least in the sense that the "democratic revolution" of which Tocqueville famously spoke requires that the ideal of aristocratic inequality be rejected on *the level of both fact and value*. To do otherwise is to defend a tradition that has no roots in the real. It is to confuse institutions and social practices that once served the common good with the permanent nature and needs of society.

The conservative liberalism of Aron repaired to the "wisdom of Montesquieu," as he often called it, to defend prudent reform and crucial political and social limitations on power, as well as to denounce the "ravages of Jacobinism" in its twentieth-century expressions. He did so as a conservative-minded liberal who "accepted the principles of democracy and the conquests of technique." His democratic conservatism repudiated the "myth of the Left" even as it recognized the partial truth and inevitable appeal of some leftist hopes and aspirations. Aron's books and journalism judiciously served to educate moderate and conservative public opinion even as he reached out to those on the Left who rejected ideological fanaticism and who were willing to make their peace with "the real."

Wisdom versus Nostalgia: Reading Burke Today

It would be a mistake to overstate the conservative features of Aron's political thought and of his role as a civic educator in the age of ideology. Like all true political philosophers, and I believe Aron is worthy of that appellation, the French political thinker saw beyond narrow partisan or ideological contestation even as he did not hesitate to express his judgments in the spirit of the "antinomic prudence" that I have outlined in this chapter. Aron's thought and vocation are in no way *reducible* to conservatism of any sort. But they are informed by a wisdom and prudence that allowed Aron, better than almost all his contemporaries, to appreciate that the true liberal is one who seeks to conserve a civilization that is broader and deeper than the "abstract moralism" proffered by the adherents to the contemporary religion of "the rights of man." At the end of his 1957 essay on "Conservatism in Industrial Societies," in a striking passage I have already cited in the opening chapter of this book, Aron suggestively contrasted two ways in which Edmund Burke's polemics against the French Revolution can be read today. It is worth returning to that passage once again: "One can read them as a definitive condemnation of political rationalism, or of ideological fanaticism. As a defense and illustration of the hierarchy of the Old Regime in its particularity, or as a demonstration that all society implies a hierarchy and only prospers in the reciprocal respect of rights and duties. Burke has either pleaded against democratic ideas, or for wisdom."

181

These words wonderfully illustrate the Burkean dimension of Aron's reflection. With this second rendering of Burke's work, we are far from the romantic Burke of Russell Kirk (who is the subject of respectful criticism in the 1957 essay) and other traditionalists and very close to the thought and voice of Raymond Aron himself.

THE UNDERLYING CONSISTENCY OF ARON'S THOUGHT

Contemporary leftist critics such as Serge Audier, who want to admire Aron and glory in May 1968 at the same time, have found solace in a fiction in which a centrist, even moderately leftist Aron transformed himself in the last fifteen years of his life into a "pessimistic" conservative at odds with the "moral progress" of contemporary European societies.[3] The real Aron was neither a pessimist nor an optimist even as he came to express grave reservations about the democratic humanitarianism that he believed substituted for political judgment in post-1968 Europe. As some of his later works such as *In Defense of Decadent Europe* testify, Aron worried about a crisis of authority in the church, army, and university and was concerned that European elites had forgotten that *virtù*—collective unity and resolve—were indispensable for the survival and well-being of liberal communities. He was the first prominent critic of the "depoliticization" of European democracy, the tendency of Europeans to abstract from the requirements of power politics—from that history that still "writes its letters in blood"—and to identify freedom with the endless expansion of social and economic rights and hedonistic self-absorption. In *The Committed Observer* (1981, 1983 for the English-language edition), Aron pleaded with his contemporaries to "remember that individuals in democracy are at once private persons and citizens." A liberal order, he insisted, is "a citizen's society and not simply one of consumers or producers." To think otherwise is to succumb to a kind of "reverse Marxism."

At the end of his life, Aron underestimated the fragility of Soviet Communism and overestimated the *virtù* (however perverse) that such a system could draw upon. Nonetheless, he had legitimate reasons to fear that the decadence of the West might "unnaturally" preserve the life of a superannuated despotism based on the twin pillars of violence and the lie. His warnings to the West therefore remain relevant long after the demise of ideological despotisms of the Soviet sort.

Aron provides a still relevant example of an intellectual in democratic life who admirably transcended the modern intellectual's preoccupation with "commitment" as an end in itself, a preoccupation often fueled by debilitating fear of appearing insufficiently progressive. This is one final lesson in civic and intellectual courage to be learned from Aron's model of responsible engagement in democratic public life. It is a particularly instructive example of a wise and humane "conservative liberalism" at work in the great political and ideological drama of modern times.

Notes

Chapter 1: Tocqueville and the Conservative Foundations of the Liberal Order

1. For unconvincing portraits of Burke as a slow-motion progressive, see Sam Tanenhaus, *The Death of Conservatism* (New York: Random House, 2009); and the final pages of Jeffrey Hart, *The Making of the American Conservative Mind: National Review and Its Times* (Wilmington, DE: ISI Books, 2005).

Chapter 2: Beyond Nihilism

1. Mark Lilla, *The Stillborn God: Religion, Politics, and the Modern West* (New York: Knopf, 2007).

2. See Manent's remarkably suggestive discussion of the "organization of separations" in *A World beyond Politics?: A Defense of the Nation-State*, translated by Marc LePain (Princeton: Princeton University Press, 2006), 10–20.

3. See Jean Bethke Elshtain, *Sovereignty: God, State, and Self* (New York: Basic Books, 2008), especially the chapter entitled "Self-Sovereignty: Moralism, Nihilism, and Existential Isolation."

Chapter 4: Churchill on Civilization and Its Discontents

1. In this section of the chapter I have drawn upon a few paragraphs in my article "Moral Principle and Realistic Judgment" from James W. Muller, ed., *Churchill's "Iron Curtain" Speech Fifty Years Later* (Columbia, MO: University of Missouri Press, 1999), 69–81.

CHAPTER 5: 1968 AND THE MEANING OF DEMOCRACY

1. De Gaulle's "Discours du 30 mai 1968" is widely available on the Internet.

2. See the illuminating conversation with Chantal Delsol ("*Le père chasse de sa maison*") dated May 15, 2008, at www.libertepolitique.fr.

3. See Dominique Schnapper, "Relativisme," *Commentaire* 31, no. 121 (2008), 126–30. An English-version language of this text appeared in the March/April 2009 issue of *Society.*

CHAPTER 6: CONSERVATISM, DEMOCRACY, AND FOREIGN POLICY

1. Charles Kesler, "Democracy and the Bush Doctrine," *Claremont Review of Books*, Vol. 5, No. 1 (Winter 2004), 18.

2. Pierre Manent, *A World beyond Politics?: A Defense of the Nation-State*, translated by Marc LePain (Princeton, NJ: Princeton University Press, 2006), viii. The quotations are drawn from Manent's "Preface to the American Edition."

CHAPTER 7: THE TOTALITARIAN SUBVERSION OF MODERNITY

1. The quotations at the opening of this paragraph are from Solzhenitsyn's *Rebuilding Russia* (New York: Farrar, Straus, and Giroux, 1991) and from "We have ceased to see the Purpose," his September 14, 1993, address to the International Academy of Philosophy. This speech served as the Russian writer's valedictory address to the West before his return to his native Russia in the spring of 1994.

2. On the mendacious character of these claims—and other such as that of anti-Semitism—see Daniel J. Mahoney, "Traducing Solzhenitsyn," *First Things*, August-September 2004, 14–17.

3. French and English versions of Solzhenitsyn's remarks of December 13, 2000, upon receiving the Grand Prize of the *Académie des sciences morales et politiques* are available on the Academy's website at www.asmp.fr/prix_fondations/grand_prix_aca_2000.htm.

CHAPTER 8: "MORAL INSANITY" AND "MORAL SQUALOR"

1. See Michael Burleigh, *Blood and Rage: A Cultural History of Terrorism* (New York: HarperCollins, 2008).

2. The reader should begin with Michael Burleigh, *The Third Reich: A New History* (New York: Hill and Wang, 2000). This work is a prolegomenon to Burleigh's trilogy on modern "political religions": *Earthly Powers: The Clash of Religion and Politics in Europe from the French Revolution to the Great War* (New York: HarperCollins, 2005), *Sacred Causes: The Clash of Religion and Politics from the Great War to the War on Terror* (New York: HarperCollins, 2007), and *Blood and Rage*. See Daniel J. Mahoney, "Michael Burleigh as Historian of 'Political Religion,'" *Intercollegiate Review*, Spring 2008, 42–52.

CHAPTER 9: RAYMOND ARON'S MODEL OF DEMOCRATIC CONSERVATISM

1. For such a discussion, see the opening chapter of my book *The Liberal Political Science of Raymond Aron: A Critical Introduction* (Lanham, MD: Rowman & Littlefield, 1992).

2. I am indebted to the Aron scholar Franciszek Draus for highlighting the significance of this passage.

3. See Audier's strident, "politically correct" polemic *La pensée anti-68*, Paris, 2008.

Suggested Readings

Chapter 1: Tocqueville and the Conservative Foundations of the Liberal Order

Aron, Raymond. *Essai sur les libertés*. Paris: Hachette Pluriel, 1965, 1998.

Bruckberger, R. L. *Images of America: A Political, Industrial, and Social Portrait*. With a new introduction by Daniel J. Mahoney. New Brunswick, NJ: Transaction, 2009.

Burke, Edmund. *Further Reflections on the Revolution in France*. Edited by Daniel E. Ritchie. Indianapolis, IN: Liberty Fund, 1992.

Ceaser, James W. *Reconstructing America: The Symbol of America in Modern Thought*. New Haven, CT: Yale University Press, 1997. Chapter 6 of the book contains the best available discussion of what was at stake in the Tocqueville-Gobineau exchange.

Epstein, Joseph. *Alexis de Tocqueville: Democracy's Guide*. New York: HarperCollins/Atlas Books, 2006.

Manent, Pierre. *Tocqueville and the Nature of Democracy*. Foreword by Harvey C. Mansfield, translated by John Waggoner. Lanham, MD: Rowman & Littlefield, 1996. The French edition, originally published by Julliard in 1982, was rereleased in Gallimard's "Tel" series in 2006.

Rahe, Paul A. *Soft Despotism, Democracy's Drift: Montesquieu, Rousseau, Tocqueville, and the Modern Prospect*. New Haven, CT: Yale University Press, 2009. Rahe's erudite book combines a valuable reading of Tocqueville with a perhaps excessive identification of contemporary democratic life with tutelary despotism.

Welsh, Cheryl B., editor. *The Cambridge Companion to Tocqueville.* New York: Cambridge University Press, 2006. In the opening pages of this chapter I draw upon Pierre Manent's article ("Tocqueville, Political Philosopher") from this volume.

Tocqueville's Writings

Tocqueville, Alexis de. *Democracy in America.* Translated, edited, and with an introduction by Harvey C. Mansfield and Delba Winthrop. Chicago: University of Chicago Press, 2000.

Tocqueville, Alexis de. *The European Revolution and Correspondence with Gobineau.* Edited and translated by John Lukacs. Garden City, NY: Doubleday Anchor, 1959.

Tocqueville, Alexis de. *The Old Regime and the Revolution, Volume 1.* Edited and with an introduction and critical apparatus by François Furet and Françoise Melonio, translated by Alan S. Kahan. Chicago: University of Chicago Press, 1988.

Tocqueville, Alexis de. *Selected Letters on Politics and Society.* Edited by Roger Boesche, translated by James Toupin and Roger Boesche. Berkeley and Los Angeles, CA: University of California Press, 1985.

Tocqueville, Alexis de. *Tocqueville and Beaumont on Social Reform.* Edited and translated with an introduction by Seymour Drescher. New York: Harper Torchbooks, 1968. This excellent volume contains Tocqueville's "Memoir on Pauperism" (1835) as well as his "Speech on the Right to Work" (1848).

Chapter 2: Beyond Nihilism

Aron, Raymond. *The Opium of the Intellectuals.* With a new introduction by Harvey C. Mansfield. Foreword by Daniel J. Mahoney and Brian C. Anderson. New Brunswick, NJ Transaction, 2003. Aron's 1956 essay "Fanaticism, Prudence, and Faith" appears as an appendix in this volume.

Brownson, Orestes. *The American Republic: Its Constitution, Tendencies, and Destiny.* With a new introduction by Peter Augustine Lawler. Wilmington, DE: ISI Books, 2003. Brownson's brilliant, idiosyncratic reflection on American republicanism was first published in 1865.

Constant, Benjamin. *Principles of Politics Applicable to All Governments.* Translated by Dennis O'Keefe. Indianapolis, IN: Liberty Fund, 2003.

Hancock, Ralph. "Back to Where We Started or The New Hobbism Comes Out." *Perspectives on Political Science.* Winter 2009, Vol. 38. No. 1, 13–15.

Hobbes, Thomas. *Leviathan: On the Matter, Forme, and Power of a Commonwealth Ecclesiastical and Civil.* Selected and with an introduction by Richard S. Peters. Edited by Michael Oakeshott. New York: Collier, 1962.

Jouvenel, Bertrand de. *Sovereignty: An Inquiry into the Political Good.* Translated by J. F. Huntington with a foreword by Daniel J. Mahoney and David M. DesRosiers. Indianapolis, IN: Liberty Fund, 1997.

Kolnai, Aurel. *Privilege and Liberty and Other Essays in Political Philosophy.* Edited and with an introduction by Daniel J. Mahoney. With a foreword by Pierre Manent. Lanham, MD: Lexington Books, 1999.

Lilla, Mark. *The Stillborn God: Religion, Politics, and the Modern West.* New York: Knopf, 2007.

Manent, Pierre. *The City of Man.* Translated by Marc A. LePain. Princeton, NJ: Princeton University Press, 1998.

Manent, Pierre. *Enquête sur la démocratie.* With an Avant-propos by Jean-Vincent Holeindre. Paris: Gallimard, 2007.

Manent, Pierre. *Modern Liberty and Its Discontents.* Edited and translated by Daniel J. Mahoney and Paul Seaton. With an introduction by Daniel J. Mahoney. Lanham, MD: Rowman & Littlefield, 1998. The 1993 essay "Christianity and Democracy" can be found on 97–115.

Polanyi, Michael. *Knowing and Being.* Edited by Marjorie Grene. Chicago: University of Chicago Press, 1969. The 1960 Eddington Lecture, "Beyond Nihilism," can be found on 3–23.

CHAPTER 3: TAKING GREATNESS SERIOUSLY

Aron, Raymond. *The Dawn of Universal History: Selected Essays of a Witness of the Twentieth Century,* 2002. New York: Basic Books. The title essay is the final piece in the volume.

Churchill, Winston. *Thoughts and Adventures.* Edited with a new introduction by James W. Muller. Wilmington, DE: ISI Books, 2009.

James W. Muller's introduction provides a particularly thoughtful account of Churchill's reflection on the problem that modern science and "mass effects" pose to the moral and political responsibility of human beings.

Faulkner, Robert. *The Case for Greatness: Honorable Ambition and Its Critics.* New Haven: Yale University Press, 2008.

Gaulle, Charles de. *The Enemy's House Divided.* Translated, annotated, and with an introduction by Robert Eden. Chapel Hill, NC: University of North Carolina Press, 2002. De Gaulle's book, perhaps his most revealing and "philosophic," was first published in 1924 when the French officer (and future statesman) was thirty-four years of age.

Jaffa, Harry V. *Statesmanship: Essays in Honor of Winston Churchill.* Durham, NC: Carolina Academic Press, 1981. Strauss's spontaneous remarks on hearing of the death of Churchill serve as the epigraph to the book.

Johnson, Paul. *Heroes: From Alexander the Great and Julius Caesar to Churchill and de Gaulle.* New York: Harper, 2007.

Mahoney, Daniel J. *De Gaulle: Statesmanship, Grandeur, and Modern Democracy.* New Brunswick, NJ: Transaction, 2000.

Tocqueville. *Democracy in America.* The chapter "On Some Tendencies Particular to Historians in Democratic Centuries" (Vol. 2, Part I, chapter 20) is Tocqueville's most incisive reflection on the limits of the purely "democratic" understanding of historical causation.

CHAPTER 4: CHURCHILL ON CIVILIZATION AND ITS DISCONTENTS

Berlin, Isaiah. *The Proper Study of Mankind: An Anthology of Essays.* Edited by Henry Hardy and Roger Hauscheer. New York: Farrar, Strauss, and Giroux, 1998. Berlin's essay "Winston Churchill in 1940," originally published in the *Atlantic Monthly* in 1949, is an elegantly unabashed articulation of Churchill's "Periclean" qualities during the crucial year when Britain stood alone.

Kissinger, Henry. *Diplomacy.* New York: Simon & Schuster, 1994.

Lukacs, John. *Blood, Toil, Tears, and Sweat: The Dire Warning: Churchill's First Speech as Prime Minister.* New York: Basic Books, 2008.

Morgenthau, Hans J. *Politics Among Nations: The Struggle for Power and Peace.* New York: Knopf, 1968.

Pangle, Thomas L. *The Ennobling of Democracy: The Challenge of the Postmodern Age.* Baltimore, MD: Johns Hopkins Press, 1992. I am indebted to Pangle's lucid discussion of the 1938 "Civilization" speech in his essay "The Challenge From and For Europe."

Valiunas, Algis. *Churchill's Military Histories: A Rhetorical Study.* Lanham, MD: Rowman & Littlefield, 2002. This book stands out for its thoughtful and suggestive treatment of Churchill as writer, historian, and political philosopher.

Churchill's Writings

Churchill, Winston S. *Never Give In! The Best of Winston Churchill's Speeches.* Selected by his grandson Winston S. Churchill. New York: Hyperion, 2003.

Churchill, Winston. *Blood, Sweat, and Tears.* New York: G. P. Putnam's Sons, 1941. The 1938 speech on "Civilization" can be found on 45–46.

Churchill, Winston. *The Gathering Storm. Vol. 1. of The Second World War.* Boston: Houghton Mifflin Company, 1948.

Churchill, Winston. *Blood, Toil, Tears, and Sweat: The Great Speeches.* Edited by David Cannadine. New York: Penguin, 2007.

CHAPTER 5: 1968 AND THE MEANING OF DEMOCRACY

Aron, Raymond. *The Elusive Revolution.* New York: Praeger, 1969. The French original, *La révolution introuvable*, is included in the best available anthology of Aron's writings, *Penser la liberté, penser la démocratie* (Paris: Gallimard, 2005), 605–748.

Aron, Raymond. *Thinking Politically: A Liberal in the Age of Ideology.* With a new introduction by Daniel J. Mahoney and Brian C. Anderson. New Brunswick, NJ: Transaction, 1997. See 207–11 for a particularly lively exchange with two former *soixante-huitards* on the meaning and import of the May events. I am indebted to the chronology of events provided by Aron in this work.

Audier, Serge. *La pensée anti-68: Essai sur les origines d'une restauration intellectuelle.* Paris: La Découverte, 2008. Audier's book is an egregious effort to claim Aron for the leftist cause and to discredit all criticisms of May '68 and the liberationist/humanitarian ethos to which it gave rise.

Besançon, Alain. "Souvenirs et réflexions sur Mai 68." *Commentaire.* Été 2008, 31, no. 122, 507–20.

Ferry, Luc, and Renault, Alain. *La pensée 68.* Paris: Gallimard, 1988, 2008. Gallimard reissued the book for the fortieth anniversary of May 1968.

Tocqueville, Alexis de. *Recollections: The French Revolution of 1848.* Edited by J. P. Mayer and A. P. Kerr. Introduction by J. P. Mayer. With a new introduction by Fernand Braudel. Translated by George Lawrence. New Brunswick, NJ: Transaction, 1987, 1970. Tocqueville's book was completed in 1851 but was published posthumously in 1893. Tocqueville and Aron share in common an allergy to revolutionary romanticism and an acute awareness of the limits of "literary politics" in all its forms.

Chapter 6: Conservatism, Democracy, and Foreign Policy

Fukuyama, Francis. *America at the Crossroads: Democracy, Power, and the Neoconservative Legacy.* New Haven, CT: Yale University Press, 2006.

Kesler, Charles. "Democracy and the Bush Doctrine." *Claremont Review of Books.* Vol. 5, No. 1, Winter 2004, 18.

Kolnai, Aurel. *Privilege and Liberty and Other Essays in Political Philosophy.* Edited and with an introduction by Daniel J. Mahoney. With a foreword by Pierre Manent. Lanham, MD: Lexington Books, 1999. Kolnai's 1949 essay on "The Meaning of the Common Man'" can be found on 63–104. The opening quotation from this essay (see p. 64) beautifully articulates the thesis of this book.

Kristol, Irving. *Neoconservatism: The Autobiography of an Idea.* Chicago: Ivan R. Dee, 1999. The essays in this volume capture Kristol's ambivalence about the "democratic idea" in its pure or unadulterated form.

Strauss, Leo. *On Tyranny.* Revised and Expanded Edition. Including the Strauss-Kojève Correspondence. Edited by Victor Gourevitch and Michael S. Roth. Chicago: University of Chicago Press, 1949, 2000.

Zakaria, Fareed. *The Future of Freedom: Illiberal Democracy at Home And Abroad.* New York: W. W. Norton and Company, 2003, 2007.

CHAPTER 7: THE TOTALITARIAN SUBVERSION OF MODERNITY

Mahoney, Daniel J. *Aleksandr Solzhenitsyn: The Ascent from Ideology.* Lanham, MD: Rowman & Littlefield, 2001.

Winthrop, Delba. "Solzhenitsyn: Emerging from Under the Rubble." *Independent Journal of Philosophy.* Issue 4 (1984), 91–101.

Solzhenitsyn's Writings

Solzhenitsyn, Aleksandr. *East and West.* New York: Harper Perennial Library, 1980. This volume includes both the "Letter to the Soviet Leaders" (1973) and Janis Sapiets's 1979 BBC interview with Solzhenitsyn.

Solzhenitsyn, Aleksandr. *From Under the Rubble.* Translated by A. M. Brock, Milada Haigh, Marita Sapiets, Hilary Sternberg, and Harry Willetts under the direction of Michael Scammell. With an introduction by Max Hayward. Washington, DC: Regnery Gateway, 1975, 1981.

Solzhenitsyn, Aleksandr. *Rebuilding Russia: Reflections and Tentative Proposals.* Translated and annotated by Alexis Klimoff. New York: Farrar, Straus, and Giroux, 1991.

Solzhenitsyn, Aleksandr. *The Solzhenitsyn Reader: New and Essential Writings, 1947–2005.* Edited by Edward E. Ericson Jr. and Daniel J. Mahoney. Wilmington, DE: ISI Books, 2006. The 1978 Harvard address, the 1993 address to the International Academy of Philosophy in Liechtenstein ("We have ceased to see the Purpose"), the selections from *Russia in Collapse,* and chapter 27 of *April 1917* are among the texts cited in this chapter that can be found in this comprehensive selection of Solzhenitsyn's belletristic and prose writings. *The Solzhenitsyn Reader* includes many "early" and "late" writings of Solzhenitsyn that appear in English in that volume for the first time as well as the Russian writer's most significant essays and speeches.

Solzhenitsyn, Aleksandr. *November 1916: The Red Wheel Knot II.* Translated by H. T. Willetts. New York: Farrar, Straus, and Giroux, 1999.

Chapter 8: "Moral Insanity" and "Moral Squalor"

Burleigh, Michael. *Blood and Rage: A Cultural History of Terrorism.* New York: HarperCollins, 2008.

Cooper, Barry. *New Political Religions, or An Analysis of Modern Terrorism.* Columbia, MO: University of Missouri Press, 2004.

Dostoevsky, Fyodor. *Demons.* Translated by Richard Pevear and Larissa Volokhonsky. New York: Vintage Books, 1994.

Laqueur, Walter, ed. *Voices of Terror: Manifestos, Writings, and Manuals of Al Qaeda, Hamas, and Other Terrorists From Around the World and Throughout the Ages.* New York: Reed Press, 2004.

Chapter 9: Raymond Aron's Model of Democratic Conservatism

Aron, Raymond. *Espoir et peur du siècle.* Paris: Plon, 1957.

Aron, Raymond. *Thinking Politically.* This volume includes the English-language edition of *Le spectateur engagé (The Committed Observer)*, several interviews with Aron from the 1970s, and the English-language version of "Democratic States and Totalitarian States: An Address to the French Philosophical Society, June 17, 1939."

Aron, Raymond. *Peace and War: A Theory of International Relations.* With a new introduction by Daniel J. Mahoney and Brian C. Anderson. New Brunswick, NJ: Transaction, 2003. Originally published in English by Doubleday (1966).

Aron, Raymond. *Penser la liberté, penser la démocratie.* Paris: Gallimard, 2005. This 1,814-page volume is by far the most comprehensive edition of Aron's foundational texts and includes *L'homme contre les tyrans* as well as the June 17, 1939, address to the French Philosophical Society.

Mahoney, Daniel J. *The Liberal Political Science of Raymond Aron: A Critical Introduction.* Lanham, MD: Rowman & Littlefield, 1992.

Acknowledgments

This book could not have been written without the generous support, encouragement, and insight provided by friends. I am particularly indebted to Paul Seaton, who read every chapter and provided indispensable suggestions along the way. Pierre Manent, Philippe Bénéton, Ralph C. Hancock, Peter A. Lawler, and James Ceaser have been precious interlocutors on the broad themes of this book for many years now. Discerning readers will see their influence refracted in the pages of this book even if the aforementioned might approach things in a somewhat different way. I am also grateful to Marc Guerra.

Four of the chapters in this book—including the opening two, the theoretical core of the book—appear in these pages for the first time. The remaining chapters were expressly written with this book in mind and have been significantly revised for inclusion in it. I would like to thank the editors of *City Journal*, the *Intercollegiate Review*, the *St. Austin Review, Orbis, On Principle*, and *Society* for permission to draw upon pieces that originally appeared in the pages of those journals.

I owe a special word of thanks to Jeremy Beer, former editor in chief of ISI Books, who from the beginning appreciated the significance of this project, and Jed Donahue, his successor at ISI Books, who has been extremely supportive and who has brought his impressive editorial expertise to bear on my manuscript. Thanks are also due to Bill Kauffman who edited the manuscript with a light but skillful touch.

Last but not least, I am also indebted to the Earhart Foundation of Ann Arbor, Michigan, and its president, Ingrid Gregg, for a generous grant that provided ample leisure to move forward with this book. The Earhart Foundation has been a consistent supporter of a humane scholarship of liberty. The confidence of the foundation in my work is both acknowledged and deeply appreciated.

Daniel J. Mahoney
Worcester, Massachusetts
July 12, 2010

Index